RISING ABOVE COGNITIVE ERRORS:

IMPROVING SEARCHES, EVALUATIONS, AND DECISION-MAKING

RESOURCES FOR MEDICAL, LAW, & BUSINESS SCHOOLS AND COLLEGES & UNIVERSITIES

JoAnn Moody, PhD, JD
National Consultant in Faculty Recruitment, Retention, & Mentorship

Cognitive scientists are proving that many of the selection and evaluation processes we undertake on a daily basis are alarmingly "contaminated," despite our good intentions. The contaminants—generically termed "cognitive shortcuts and errors"—are present as we gather and sort through information, interpret it, and reach decisions about: candidates for jobs, tenure/promotion, and contract renewals; applications for grants; nominations for awards and leadership posts; and colleagues' and students' professional and academic performances, their mastery of new concepts and skills, and their publications, exhibits, and other displays of mastery and creativity.

During these intense evaluation processes, most of us *unwittingly* commit a variety of errors and automatically take shortcuts. A chronic one, regularly showing up in our personal and professional lives, is the confusion between causation and correlation. Unfortunately, there are many more confusions! If we are rushed and distracted, then cognitive errors and shortcuts demonstrably multiply. When those involved in evaluation and decision-making are not coached and not given the opportunity to be thorough, deliberate, and self-correcting, then dysfunction results.

Recognizing this danger, several law and medical schools have begun coaching their students and residents to form self-correction habits and to routinely use checklists and other safeguard protocols and reminders. Likewise senior decision-makers at colleges, universities, and professional schools (as well their gate-keeping bodies such as search committees) are receiving instruction in cognitive errors and in structural ways to minimize the errors and improve peer review. Such instruction of individuals and committees plus larger organizational change are *long* overdue.

Consider diagnoses of medical disorders. In examining and interacting with patients and reviewing lab results, practitioners must be able to resist predictable and preventable errors, including first impressions; rushing to judgment; bias based on gender or group membership; failing to factor in atypical symptoms and instead selectively choosing data that confirm one's original hunches (Dawson & Arkes; Groopman, *How Doctors Think*; Croskerry; Redelmeier; Bond).

Similarly, behavioral economists, legal and cognitive experts (such as Sunstein, Thaler, Kahneman, Greenwald, Krieger) have identified shortcuts and biases that corrupt "rational" thinking, the estimates of probabilities, and sound decision-making. Who are susceptible to these shortcuts? Lawyers, judges, juries, investors (big and small), civic leaders, politicians, Federal Reserve Bank directors, campus leaders, and of course the general public. For instance, how one chooses to frame a problem can easily shut down open-minded exploration and foreclose certain solutions. Anchoring (that is, fierce adherence to one's first impression) will corrupt deliberations and judgments as will a number of other predictable cognitive errors.

<u>My Purpose</u>. Medical, legal, business, and academic institutions must pay more attention. Evaluators and decision-makers in these workplaces, I maintain, should become informed about the typical cognitive shortcuts and biases that can prevent their reaching fair and sound judgments or diagnoses. Once aware of these traps, the power-holders can learn, through practice, to *recognize* and then *rise above* the errors.

In Part I of this booklet, I illustrate fifteen cognitive errors and shortcuts--routinely and unwittingly made by individual evaluators and by evaluation bodies—that I have observed for decades. Then I cast light on six common structural dysfunctions within organizations that can and usually do intensify the severity of the cognitive errors.

In Part II, I set forth concrete steps for rising above or preventing these errors together with concrete steps for reducing the organizational dysfunctions.

Part III contains several Discussion Scenarios (practice exercises). These can be used by established and emerging leaders, key committees, department chairs and deans, and indeed entire departments and schools, to hone critical-thinking and

decision-making skills. I am pleased that several national professional societies and federal agencies increasingly use the scenarios and the entire booklet in sessions at their annual meetings.

Finally at the end of the publication, you will find a summary of all errors, dysfunctions, and recommended action steps that I have presented. This summary is for the convenience of individual readers and for various leaders (provosts, faculty affairs offices, deans, chairs, chief diversity officers) who organize sessions to benefit search and other evaluation committees, departmental units, trustees, mentors, and new, established, or emerging leaders.

The Good News. With concentration and practice, most of us can learn to identify and eliminate or at least reduce predictable contaminants in evaluation processes. Recent publications by a number of cognitive psychologists and neuroscientists are suggesting *how* to do this. For years, business management experts have outlined ways to shrink organizational problems that can quickly corrupt evaluation processes. None of this is new. We already know a lot.

Out in the "field" where I do consulting work with various campuses and professional schools, I see heartening evidence that coaching, practicing, and "priming" will indeed enable faculty, administrators, and evaluation bodies to rise above sloppy decision-making. And I see that new organizational practices will shrink the likelihood of cognitive errors and biases being committed unthinkingly.

We professionals are certainly accustomed to intense concentration and constant correction and revision if we are to achieve and maintain depth in our various disciplinary fields. So too are concentration and continual revisions necessary if we are to execute fair and sound evaluations of colleagues, students, applicants, clients, patients, and others.

PART I

COGNITIVE SHORTCUTS AND ERRORS MADE BY INDIVIDUAL EVALUATORS AND DECISION-MAKERS

Most of us are probably very familiar with the basic idea of stereotyping. It's a notion that's been a part of our vocabulary for decades. You've surely heard some of the following:

Tall men make better leaders. I'm often treated as dumb because I'm blonde. Asians and Asian Americans are more innately better at math and engineering than any other ethnic group. White men can't jump. Women are emotional; men are rational. Most people, when they see me or others in wheelchairs, assume that we're all mentally handicapped. Those who can, do; those who can't, teach.

In that short list, notice that you heard negative stereotypes about some groups but also positive stereotypes about others. This is one important fact to remember: stereotypes can be positive as well as negative. If a positive stereotype surrounds a certain favored group, then members of that group are very likely to realize hidden profits—such as, getting the benefit of the doubt about their performance, their intentions, or their potential. By contrast, if a negative stereotype surrounds a disfavored group, members from that group are very likely to be presented with extra penalties—

such as never getting or hardly ever getting the benefit of the doubt.

A stereotype can be defined as a broad generalization about a particular group and the assumption that a member of the group embodies the generalized traits of that group. Dozens of experts--brain specialists, social scientists, cultural anthropologists, lawyers and law professors, courtroom judges, medical diagnosticians, and management experts--are discovering how stereotypes and other contaminants pervade our cognitive processes of evaluating and judging. Take a few moments to review www.implicit.harvard.edu (constructed by [*look up*] Professors Greenwald, Banaji, and Noviks). Also check the findings of experts listed in my References, such as Bauer and Baltes; Biernat; Blair and Banaji; Delgado; Foschi; Fried; Greenwald; Groopman; Kahneman; Kanter; Kobrynowicz and Biernat; Kunda, Sinclair, and Griffin; Martell, Lane, and Emrich; Martell; McIntosh; Mervis; Moskowitz, Gollwitzer, and Wasel; Nahavandi and Malekzadeh; Pinker; Rosser; Sagaria; Sanchirico; Steele and Aronson; Sturm and Guinier; Trix and Psenka; Valian; Wenneras and Wold; C.G. and C.L. Williams; Wilson and Brekke.)

Stereotyping (both negative and positive) is one of the most widespread cognitive errors that undermines many evaluation processes. After I discuss stereotyping and its significant role in professional life, I will move on to name and illustrate a baker's dozen of other errors and lapses.

1. Cognitive Error: Negative Stereotype.
First, let me illustrate how negative stereotypes and extra penalties can play. And then I'll switch to positive stereotypes and the hidden profits they often produce for certain people working at professional schools, colleges, and universities.

Listen to what Princeton historian Nell Painter has to say: "Intellectually, any woman and any black person must prove that she or he is not dumb. . . . The phrase 'qualified white man' simply does not exist." Painter, of African-American descent, calls it "tiresome in the extreme" to be made to feel as if you are always being evaluated and that your qualifications and achievements are always suspect. Even attending social gatherings—where one is "always on show, always standing for *The Negro*—saps one's energy" (Reiss, pp. 6-7).

As one minority professor on a majority campus put it, "Man, from the day we're hired until the day we're retired, we are on probation!" (quoted in Moore and Wagstaff, p. 9). Can it be any wonder that many women and minority faculty with whom I work often lament that they are never given the benefit of the doubt, that they are always "on stage" and feel they are being judged? Sociologist Lois Benjamin found that almost all of the one hundred of African-American professionals she interviewed for her book *The Black Elite* felt they were indeed on "perennial probation" and had to prove themselves twice as accomplished as majority colleagues in academe, law, and medicine (Benjamin, p. 28; also see Cooper and Stevens).

Studies have shown that peer reviewers at the Swedish Research Council almost always assumed that women applicants for post-doctoral grants possessed less scientific competence than men applicants with the *same* credentials and qualifications. To be competitive, the women had to be extraordinary. They had to have "published three extra papers" in high-impact journals like *Nature* and *Science* or "20 extra papers" in excellent but less prestigious journals. In short, a female applicant "had to be 2.5 times more productive than the average male applicant to receive the same competence score as he" (Wenneras and Wold, "Nepotism and Sexism"; also see Rosser, *The Science Glass Ceiling*). The ratio of 2.5 to 1 is astounding!

What is the negative stereotype being described in these quotations? *It is, of course, the presumption of incompetence*—and this presumption endures and endures even in the face of considerable accomplishments and positive evidence. A recent internal survey of University of Michigan faculty revealed that women and minority professors at the Big Ten University frequently felt they were discriminated against, scrutinized far more than majority professors, and undervalued as intellectuals. A number of European-American male faculty members at Michigan agreed that they too had seen such undervaluing and intense scrutiny of women and minority colleagues.

To beat back the negative presumption calls for exceptional endurance. New Mexico State University Professor Herman Garcia has joked: progress will be reached when minorities throughout academia can save energy and feel as relaxed "about being mediocre" as many majorities now seem to feel (quoted in Padilla, p. 156).

A similar point is made by Joan Steitz, Professor of Molecular Biophysics and Biochemistry at Yale University. Women "superstars" in predominantly male departments, she observes, seem to have an easier time than do "sort of average" women who are bunched in the middle with "most of their male colleagues." Steitz believes that women, unlike men, seem to have a difficult time in the middle being accepted as equal colleagues and given fair and full recognition for their accomplishments (quoted in "Tomorrow's Professor"

4

Listserve operated by Professor Richard Reis and headquartered at Stanford University). To borrow a splendid quip attributed to former Congresswoman Bella Abzug, "Our struggle today is not to have a female Einstein get appointed as an assistant professor. It is for a woman *schlemiel* to get as quickly promoted as a male *schlemiel*."

For those surrounded by a negative stereotype "far more evidence is required for a judge to be certain that an individual possesses an *unexpected* attribute"—in this case, the unexpected attribute is competence while the expected attribute is incompetence (Biernat, p. 1020; see also Sagaria on filters applied differently to different groups).

University of Pittsburgh Law Professor Richard Delgado notes that when the archetypal academic search committee is seeking a new colleague and after several months of work has not located the "superhuman, mythic figure who is Black or Hispanic," then the committee turns to a non-mythic, *average* candidate who is almost always "white, male, and straight." The committee has confidence that the decision they are reaching is a sound one: this is because the lower standard of evidence--applied to a positively stereotyped person—is being unwittingly used (Delgado, p. 265).

An exhaustive study--of over 300 letters of recommendation used in hiring and promotion processes at a large medical school--uncovered significant stereotyping. Competent female faculty members were professionally underestimated and described as caring, refreshing, and diligent. By contrast, competent male faculty members were praised for their research brilliance and career achievements. A 2009 study by Rice University researchers found the same pattern in 624 letters of recommendation for

applicants seeking junior faculty positions at a research university (Madera, Hebl, and Martin). By the way, the medical letters were written by heads of departments; 85 percent of the heads were male.

The two anthropologists who conducted the medical study issue these four warnings to academics involved in the gate-keeping processes of screening, hiring, making awards, and reviewing candidates for tenure and promotion: 1) double-check and eradicate from their own verbal and written evaluations superficial assumptions related to gender schema; 2) be on guard against omitting essential topics (such as concrete career achievements) that are related to gender schema; 3) make sure that colleagues understand how the evaluations of applicants may be typically positively biased towards males and negatively prejudiced towards females; 4) coach female colleagues on how they can insure that department chairs evaluate their individual promise and professional accomplishments rather than fall back on belittling gender stereotypes (Trix and Psenka).

I will give Harvard cognitive scientist Steven Pinker the last word about negative stereotyping. He warns, "If subjective decisions about people, such as admissions, hiring, credit, and salaries, are based in part on group-wide averages, they will conspire to make the rich richer and the poor poorer." Here is one of his illustrations of circularity: financial managers often treat African Americans as poor credit risks, "which makes them less likely to succeed, which makes them poorer credit risks" (p. 206).

2. Cognitive Error: Positive Stereotype.

Now let's turn to positive stereotypes and to the experiences of those who enjoy such a halo. As you would guess, those with a halo are *presumed to be competent and bona fide.* They will not bump up against implicit quotas limiting their representation in a department or on a campus. They will collect more positive points (so to speak) for their achievements, relative to those coping with a negative stereotype. For instance, those with the positive stereotype can win professional society or book awards and not have to endure whispers that their work is actually *"terribly over-rated."*

A European-American professor, Frederick Frank, discloses that "while I worked like a Trojan to earn my way in this life, I nevertheless assert that a good measure of my success" results from societal perception. This professor is surrounded by the favorable stereotype of being competent. In such an advantageous position, he is sure he has gotten "breaks" and at times received "more positive evaluations" of his job performance "than he expected or deserved." "I try to be grateful," he says (Frank, p. 148).

Expressing similar gratitude, Management Professor Peter Couch admits that his being a white male has brought him "extra" points and extra opportunities at every stage of his academic career. "I have always found myself in a world of opportunities—opportunities that I [naively] thought were available to anyone energetic and capable" (Couch, quoted in Gallos and Ramsey, 21).

These extra points are critically important. They mount up and can create a competitive advantage. Computer modeling experts have shown how even a tiny positive bias (of 1%, for instance) affecting your job performance and reputation is very significant. That tiny bias can help you accumulate more points over a much shorter time--and in effect speed up the recognition

and promotions you receive (see Valian; Martell, Lane, and Emrich).

What about job performance in the classroom? As educators, it seems that majority males are granted not only more authority and acceptance but also more leeway to make mistakes in the classroom. In studies by Pennsylvania State University Professor Frances Rains, she comes to describe such authority and leeway as "concealed profits" that majority males usually enjoy. Members of this group reap these profits because students view them as the norm and as automatically entitled to intellectual authority and deference inside and outside the classroom (Rains, p. 53).

These illustrations point out that the clear and daily benefits of belonging to a group that is viewed as competent. Members of such a positively regarded group, according to a number of experts, are likely to:

- receive the benefit of the doubt if there is ambiguous evidence about how well they performed or behaved
- receive more points for their achievements
- find that their points accumulate faster and produce a sturdy base of successes
- be assured that their successes are unlikely to be questioned or suspected
- not face a quota system that restricts them to token representation (meaning one of a few) as well as to marginal power in an organization
- and, finally, they will enjoy greater deference inside and outside their traditional venues, whether that is the college classroom, the laboratory, the boardroom, the courtroom, the operating room, or the legislature.

But what about one's treatment in a non-traditional venue? When a man unconventionally enters a female-dominated profession such as nursing or librarianship, he will certainly be the token (meaning he is the only one or one of a few "others" who are different from the rest). A solo or one of a few, according to organizational experts, usually occupies a stressful and awkward position because those in the majority give skewed attention to the solo and often misinterpret his/her real motives and performance (Yoder, Kanter). Yet this man, albeit unusual in nursing or library work, nevertheless brings his higher status and positive stereotype of competence with him. Instead of being devalued and hitting a glass ceiling (as a woman, for instance, in science and engineering would almost certainly experience), the male solo will typically find himself on a "glass escalator" that somehow brings quick recognition, promotion, and a corner office as a dean and director (C.L. Williams). In short, those assigned a positive stereotype will receive substantial hidden profits that advance them on a cumulative basis in both traditional and non-traditional settings. Those assigned a negative stereotype will be dealt extra penalties and taxes that set them back on a cumulative basis (see C.L. Williams, C.G. Williams, Steele and Aronson, McIntosh, Moody, Valian, Rosser, MIT Report).

How do negative and positive stereotypes arise? In another publication, I point primarily to political power. Synthesizing the work of dozens of anthropologists, political scientists, economists, historians, novelists, and sociologists, I outline why in this country *non-immigrants* (those whose ancestors started out in this country as the conquered--incorporated by *force, not choice*) are usually branded with long-lasting negative stereotypes and lower status. These groups include Native Americans, African Americans, Puerto Rican Americans, and Mexican Americans.

By contrast, voluntary immigrants in the widest sense of that term usually enjoy higher status and expectations that they will succeed in attaining the American dream. They benefit because they and their ancestors exercised varying degrees of *choice* as they entered the country. These groups include: members of the dominant European-American group; Asians and Asian Americans who are now treated as honorary whites (Wu, Lopez, Takaki); and international visitors and new immigrants. What about European-American women's status and treatment? These will vary, largely depending on whether the women are trying to enter and succeed in fields traditionally closed to them (Moody, Chapter 2, *Faculty Diversity*).

A Segue. Having discussed negative and positive stereotypes at length, I now will move more quickly to identify and illustrate a number of other cognitive errors and shortcuts. I do want to admit that one or another of these errors will almost converge, at times, with a related one. Yet I have found it helpful in my consulting work to struggle to keep all the errors separate and distinct, especially during the introductory phase.

3. Cognitive Error: Raising the Bar.
This error, related to negative stereotyping, involves raising requirements for a job or an award <u>during</u> the very process of evaluation. The raising is felt to be necessary because of the decision-maker's realization that the candidate is a member of a group thought to be incompetent and suspect. You may hear:

Say, don't we need more writing samples from Latorya? I know we asked for only three law review articles or other compositions from applicants. But I'd feel better if we had a few more in this case. I just want to sure she's really qualified.

A second instance: Another committee member agrees and says, *Well, I wish Latorya had a doctorate from Princeton or somewhere like that. Can't we decide right now that a candidate has to be from the Ivy League or maybe Berkeley? I think we can.*

My point is that raising the bar is unfair and yet unwittingly and repeatedly done in evaluations. Unfortunately, power-holders don't stop to ponder why they may be uncomfortable and why they desire both more evidence and more qualifications for one candidate but not for another.

4. Cognitive Error: Elitism.

This error involves feeling superior or wanting to feel superior. Elitism (also known as snobbery) could take this form: downgrading on the basis of the candidate's undergraduate or doctoral campuses, regional accent, dress, jewelry, social class, ethnic background, and so on (Moody, Padilla). A search committee member might complain: *She's so very Southern--I'm not sure I can stand that syrupy accent. And I always associate that kind of accent with illiteracy.* Or conversely, giving extra points on the basis of the candidate's alma mater, accent, dress, or other items can be a manifestation of elitism. A search committee member might observe about a candidate: *Isn't it nice to hear his English accent? That's worth a million to me.*

Another example: Fearing that a non-immigrant (U.S. domestic) minority colleague will somehow lessen the quality and standing of the department, a committee member might say: *Well, shouldn't we always ask if a particular hire like Dewayne is likely to bolster our place in the business school ratings wars? I think that's okay.*

Another example: *Are we sure Ricardo will be productive enough to keep up with our publishing standards? I'm not so sure.*

Elitism can, of course, prompt a committee member to feel validated because the candidate will bring some extra snob appeal. *I think Les's doctorate from Stanford is just the kind of boost in prestige that we could use around here. I see no reason why we can't take the Stanford degree at face value and forego the so-called 'weighting' of what Les has done at Stanford with what the other candidates have accomplished at their hard-scrabble places. To me, that's an awful waste of our time.*

5. Cognitive Error: First Impressions.

Probably most of us are perennially reminding ourselves to stop judging a book by its cover. Unless we remain on guard, we will unfairly make conclusions about a candidate or applicant or new acquaintance in a matter of seconds, based on whether their dress or cologne or posture or laughter or something else pleases or displeases us. Our own personal values and likes/dislikes (as opposed to our learned stereotypes about certain groups) can inordinately influence us to make fast and unexamined assumptions and even decisions about a person's worth or appeal.

For instance, you might hear a powerful gate-keeper observe: *Well, that ponytail and those blue jeans clinched it for me, as soon as I saw him walk towards us. Clearly the applicant is disrespecting us.* Responding to the same candidate at the same moment in time, a second person might observe: *I got a kick out of the ponytail and jeans. I bet he'd* be a lively person for our surgical team. Both of these rapid-fire assumptions could be fuel for sloppy decision-making about the applicant.

LOYALTY TO THE CLAN

6. Cognitive Error: The Longing to Clone.

The longing to clone (reproduce yourself or your group as nearly as you can) appears in the search process when committee members undervalue a candidate's educational credentials and career preparation to simply because they are not the same as most of those on the hiring committee. You might hear a search committee member ask: *Hey, have we ever hired anyone with a doctorate from the University of Oregon? We don't know anything about that place. No one **here** ever went to that school, did they? No way.*

Another instance of cloning: a committee member seeks candidates who resemble a colleague who has retired or died. You would hear: *I can't believe that Tony has been gone for three years now. He was the perfect colleague and tax expert. Isn't it time we found someone just like him?*

While the sentiment about missing Tony's presence is understandable, the danger comes when the committee constructs a very narrow net in order to find a Tony-like replacement and recreate the past. Casting a narrow net could do a disservice to the growth and evolution of the school and will shrink the number of qualified candidates who might be given serious consideration.

7. Cognitive Error: Good Fit/Bad Fit.

Increasingly, gate-keeping individuals and committees ponder and worry whether a candidate would be a good or bad fit for their department. While it is necessary for a job candidate to be able to meet the agreed-on needs of the department, of the students,

(and perhaps of the community) as well as possess the professional qualifications listed in the position description, this is not what is usually meant by good or bad fit. Instead, "fit" is often stretched to mean "Will I feel comfortable and culturally at ease with this new hire or will I have to spend energy to learn some new ways to relate to this hire?"

In other words, the longing to clone and to stay as a mono-culture within the department may be prompting the complaint that the candidate "just won't fit with us." The same longing to clone can appear in tenure reviews when the candidate is faulted for not being collegial. Be on guard against rampant subjectivity when the all-important question is posed: "Is this a good fit?"

You may overhear: *Well, I think Mercedes doesn't deserve tenure. We've lived with her long enough to know that she's really very, very different from the rest of us. Sure, she can do the job and do it rather well. But to be blunt, she's just not the kind of person I like to spend time with, especially socially. She's never going to become a soccer mom in this town, if you know what I mean.*

Another search example: *Timothy will stick out in our department, as I'm sure everyone here senses. Won't he be hard to relate to? He's just too different from the rest of us. We've got a bad fit here, I think. On the other hand, Jerry will be great for us. He can hit the ground running and will be able to read our minds—well, at least most of the time. That's the beauty of his coming here. He'll fit right in to everything, very fast.*

8. Cognitive Error: Provincialism.

Closely related to cloning, this error means undervaluing something outside your own province, circle, or clan. Several comprehensive studies have shown that evaluation committees often tend to trust only those letters of recommendation or external review that are written by people they personally know (Sagaria; also see Wenneras and Wold where they pinpoint the "affiliation bonus" given to applicants belonging in certain networks).

You might hear a committee member disclose: *Listen, I'm uneasy because I have never met this reference. I have a gut feeling that we shouldn't give his letter much credence. In effect, the committee member is announcing: "I trust only those from my clan or network."*

Another example: *Here's a funny, old-fashioned letter using very stilted grammar. I'm not sure we should really believe all the superlatives in this external review. The author just doesn't know how to write a letter for us. That's pretty clear, isn't it?*

DISTORTING AND IGNORING EVIDENCE

9. Cognitive Error: Extraneous Myths and Assumptions (Including "Psycho-analyzing" the Candidate)

Personal opinions and misinformation should be suspect during evaluations. So too should second-guessing or what I jokingly call "psycho-analyzing the candidate." Here are several illustrations:

- *Sally will be predictably unhappy with our harsh winters and our family-centered town. I'm certain.*
- *Really, there are no qualified women or minorities for us to hire. I wish there were. The pool is bone-dry.* (Smith, Debunking the Myths).
- *No one from Georgia Tech would want to come here. I'm positive about that. Absolutely sure.*
- *Minorities will find it too rural here. I wish we had a cosmopolitan and diverse neighborhood but we don't.*

- *This candidate will turn down our offer in an instant. Our measly salary will insult this finance whiz.*
- *This candidate will not be satisfied with a small medical school like ours, no matter what she said. I can see her thriving only at a huge research university.*

10. Cognitive Error: Wishful Thinking; Rhetoric not Evidence.

By wishful thinking, I mean not only holding to a notion in spite of overwhelming evidence to the contrary but also casually allowing this notion to cloud one's cognitive processes. A common form of wishful thinking is this: insisting that America and its colleges, universities, and professional schools operate as \a *meritocracy* where whom you know and what status and privileges you start with are immaterial.

An illustration: *There is absolutely no subjectivity involved when we seek merit and excellence in candidates. We should be <u>proud</u> that all of our grant winners have been anthropology doctorates from Yale and Harvard. After all, they're the best. Yes?*

Another instance of wishful, non-critical thinking occurs when someone insists that they or the committee are color-blind and gender-blind and therefore there is no need for them to be more careful than usual in their deliberations. *Listen, I don't really see gender or race in people. Really, I don't. It doesn't matter to me whether a job candidate is black, white, green, polka dot, or purple. Really, it doesn't. I don't see why you're asking me, of all people, to bend over backwards to recruit more and more non-majority candidates. Give me a break.*

In my book on faculty diversity, I discuss how the gender-blind and race-blind assertion is almost always a self-serving, disingenuous rhetorical plea by a majority person (for non-majorities to make such an assertion would be absurd). With this plea, the majority person seems to be claiming some sort of political innocence and otherworldly infallibility as well as disclaiming any responsibility for past or current discrimination and devaluation of women and minorities.

A number of scholars agree with Penn State professor Frances Rains that the color-blind assertion attempts to "trivialize the substance and weight of the intertwined histories of Whites and people of color" (p. 93), histories intertwined since the beginning of the U.S. democracy (also see Dahl; Fair; Guinier and Torres; Takaki; Gaertner and Dovidio; Moody). While *on the surface* the color-blind, gender-blind assertion may sound admirable, it usually plays out as a disingenuous and trivializing stance that slows down actual diversifying at schools and campuses.

Finally, I want to suggest that wishful thinking can also be illustrated when an individual is satisfied with the mere uttering of his/her opinions rather than the offering of evidence and verifiable facts. Evaluation committees must beware of members who believe that maintaining "Roger is *more* qualified and sound" is the same as proving that assertion about Roger. In fact, most of the cognitive errors being discussed in this monograph could be characterized as what happens when time-consuming digging for evidence and then careful sifting through it are *abandoned.* Instead, decision-makers allow short-cut stating of opinions, personal likes and dislikes, and stereotypes to thrive. Concomitantly, they initiate or acquiesce to a rush to judgment.

11. Cognitive Error: Self-Fulfilling Prophecy.

Some experts would prefer to call this error "channeling" which has been described as structuring our interaction with someone so that we can receive information congruent with our assumptions or so that we can avoid information incongruent with our assumptions. If you have high expectations for someone, you may unthinkingly set up situations—sometimes called *priming* the situations—so that person is likely to be spotlighted in a positive way and earn extra points. Or conversely, if you have low expectations for someone, you can easily set up situations so that these low expectations will be confirmed. For instance, you provide "fewer training opportunities" and chances for the person to shine (organizational development experts Nahavandi and Malekzadeh, p. 167).

Another instance of self-fulfilling prophecy could go this way. You believe the job candidate coming for an interview tomorrow is head and shoulders above all the other candidates. Consequently, you ask one of your most senior and well-informed colleagues to meet the candidate at the airport. Primed by this colleague, the candidate will be better prepared for issues he or she will face in the upcoming interviews and evaluation process.

Yet another illustration of self-fulfilling prophecy might occur in a situation like this. The committee has chosen three candidates to interview. In your judgment as chair of the committee, two candidates look more attractive on paper than the third. Based on your reading of the files, you decide to place personal phone calls to the two you regard as more attractive, preparing them for the upcoming campus visit and answering their questions. But you ask the *department secretary* to call the third one. It shouldn't be surprising if the third candidate doesn't

11

do as well as the others during the visit. Although this slighting of one applicant is probably unintentional, the slighting can activate the self-fulfilling prophecy.

12. Cognitive Error: Seizing a Pretext.

Metaphorically speaking, seizing a pretext is creating a smoke screen to hide one's real concerns or agenda. By seizing on a pretextual reason, a power-holder can come to the decision desired while keeping hidden or obscure the real reason for the decision.

One example: Excessive weight is assigned to something trivial, in order to justify quick dismissal of the candidate. Someone might say: *Raquel seemed so nervous during the first five minutes of her job talk. Why keep her in the running for the administrative position?* What this evaluator is really doing is setting up a superficial and false reason for a thumbs-down decision.

Another example of seizing a pretext: a tenure and promotion committee decides to "selectively exclude favorable [teaching] ratings and focus on the two courses in which a professor had difficulties" and then to use this "contrivance" as a key reason for refusing tenure to the candidate. Such a deliberate and outrageous smoke screen was uncovered by a judge in a legal case discussed in *Tenure Denied: Cases of Sex Discrimination in Academia* (AAUW, pp. 56-7). Pretextual reasons, when they go unchallenged, insure contaminated results.

13. Cognitive Error: Character over Context.

Character over context means that a judge does not consider the particular context and any extenuating circumstances within that context but instead thinks automatically that an individual's *personal* characteristics explain her or his behavior. The judge thus emphasizes character. (By the way, some social scientists would prefer to call this an "attribution" error.)

Here is the first example of character over context: A committee member might say, *Well, I didn't like the offhanded way that Walter responded to your question about his most recent public health report, at dinner last night. I mean, is he really serious about this job or not?* Here the committee member ignores the social nature of the dinner setting. Perhaps the candidate thought it would inappropriate to get into a long discussion of his research since that would be the focus of his two-hour presentation the next day. Another example of character over context: A committee member hastily concludes, *"You know, Sheila didn't seem very lively when I saw her after my 4 p.m. seminar. I don't think we want a low-energy person joining our technology-transfer team."* Here the committee person ignores the context that the interview is late in the day after a lengthy series of interviews for the applicant. That context might well have been the explanation for Sheila's behavior.

A third illustration: Over the years, various personnel and tenure review committees on a campus have noticed that women and minority instructors usually earn lower teaching evaluation ratings from students than do majority candidates. Yet very few committee members have ever checked external studies to see if group-bias and gender-bias could help explain this pattern (they do). Instead, the committees often assume that non-majority candidates are totally responsible for their lower ranking and should pay the consequences.

14. Premature Ranking/Digging In.

All too often, evaluators rush to give numerical preferences to the applicants they are considering. I often wonder if this haste-to-rank brings relief to evaluators and falsely assures them that they have now escaped both personal subjectivity and embarrassing vulnerability to cognitive errors. Perhaps they finally feel they have achieved objectivity and fairness. **Ranking, after all, gets you a number and objectivity, doesn't it?** Embracing such false precision is unfortunately what many of us indulge in.

The superficial rush to rank candidates leads evaluators to prematurely state their position (*he's clearly number one*); close their minds to new evidence; and then defend their stated position to the death. Rather than developing a pool of acceptable and qualified candidates and then comparing, contrasting, and mulling over candidates' different strengths with one's colleagues, some evaluators prefer to simplify their task.

Here is one illustration of premature ranking and digging in: *Well, I don't want to waste time here in summarizing each candidate's strengths and weaknesses, as the dean suggested. That seems to me just a useless writing exercise proposed by an overzealous former English professor. I've got enough evidence to make up my mind about who should be number one, number two, and number three. I just hope we can hire number one and not be stuck with the others.*

Another illustration: *Let's go through the categories we're using and assign points to each of the serious candidates for this job. I totally trust everyone here so you don't have to give me subtle or complicated reasons for your actions. With this approach, we quickly add up the points and we've got a decision on our first choice—all in twenty-five minutes or less.*

In other words, rushing to rank will eliminate the need for engagement with colleagues in higher-order thinking, sifting through and interpreting evidence, comparing and contrasting, and "weighting"

the importance of evidence. Rushing to rank easily leads to rushing to judgment.

15. Cognitive Error: Momentum of the Group.

If most members of an evaluation committee are favoring one candidate, then it will be more difficult for the remaining members to resist that push towards consensus. The remaining members will have to work harder to get a full hearing for other candidates. Sometimes the struggle doesn't seem to be worth it.

Here is one example: *Okay, this is the last time that I try to call attention to other worthy applicants. Come on, hear me out. Let me go over the strengths and weaknesses, as I see them, of two more promising folks. Hey, listen to me, please.*

And another example: *Stop and think. Doesn't it make you wonder why all the rest of us are behind Candidate A and you're the only holdout? Are you sure you're not just trying to make some ideological point or be a royal pain? I'm just kidding, of course.*

To Recap.

The fifteen errors and shortcuts just named are likely to be made—unwittingly and repeatedly--by individual power-holders during evaluation processes. These errors and shortcuts contaminate and undermine the credibility and equity of various evaluation reviews.

But when conditions and practices within a lab, institute, department, division, or larger organization are dysfunctional, then the severity of an individual's and a review committee's errors (and the consequences of those errors) is unfortunately magnified. I now want to spotlight bad practices frequently manifested at the organizational level that do serve as magnifiers.

ORGANIZATIONAL DYSFUNCTIONS THAT EXACERBATE COGNITIVE ERRORS AND UNSOUND EVALUATIONS

1. Organizational Dysfunction: Overloading and Rushing.

It is common to abruptly "thrust" a search committee or other evaluation entity into its complex task without adequate time to prepare or to execute with care. I have repeatedly heard this complaint from committee members. "No wonder," they tell me, "we can't think straight. No wonder that we keep reproducing ourselves year after year. No wonder that we can't manage to do active searches but just keep on doing wholesale screening out of candidates. We have a mess here."

Unfortunately it is standard procedure to rush and overwhelm evaluation committees. Cognitive errors and shortcuts, such as cloning, elitism, wishful thinking, premature ranking, and stereotyping, will thrive in frenetic situations. "When people are distracted or put under pressure to respond quickly," they become far more vulnerable to cognitive errors and "faulty decision-making," according to Pinker and a number of other cognitive scientists whose work parallels his (Pinker, p. 205; Martell).

Rather than committee members being relieved of some of their routine duties, they are usually given their search or other evaluation assignment as a distracting overload to their regular work. Not receiving extra secretarial support or assistance from the dean's office, the members and the chair struggle on their own to plow quickly through applications instead of carefully considering which candidates would bring new skills and strengths to their department or school. In short, the daunting details of the evaluation foster bad habits, shortcuts, and errors. As the dean of a school of public policy confided to me, "we're not elitist so much as we just don't have the time to look into doctoral programs at other places to see if their graduates would be good for us. We have to keep going with the places we've always relied on. It *is* a closed system."

Finally, search and other evaluation committees are sometimes hastily formed, with no regard to why members should have diverse backgrounds. Experience has shown that "the more diverse the committee, the more diverse the [job] candidates are likely to be" (Springer, AAUP). Insuring different gender and racial/ethnic perspectives in the committees' membership is a wise practice.

To provide variety, some departments routinely invite tenured professors from other departments to serve on evaluation committees as well as outside business and civic leaders and graduates of the institution. (See Moody, *Faculty Diversity*, Chapter 4). Organization-development experts encourage "divergent backgrounds and viewpoints" within groups, to stimulate unconventional approaches, greater attentiveness, and noticing of opportunities that would have otherwise been missed (Whetten and Cameron, p. 189).

2. Organizational Dysfunctions: No Coaching and No Practice.

Corporations habitually spend time and money ensuring that the managers who hire new employees are well-trained and practiced in search and interview methods. But professional schools and campuses often neglect this dimension—perhaps assuming that anyone can do a job search, just as anyone can teach. (Not true, of course.) A professor at a Midwest university observes that in the fifteen years since earning his doctorate, "even in my role as associate dean and department chairman, I have spent—are you ready?—not one hour of formal training in the best practices for hiring in academe."

One single job search can waste enormous "economic, administrative, emotional, and interpersonal resources" for the search members and the school as a whole.

When one accounts for the cost of job advertisements, for the time spent by search members, staff, and deans as they sort and review applications and support materials, for the travel expense of bringing finalists to campus for interview, then the total sum arrived at "is about the same as the first-year salary of that new faculty member (at least in the humanities)" (Dettmar, p. B8). If the new hire works in a specialty that requires scientific equipment and special resources, then the start-up cost is much higher.

What passes for preparation is woefully inadequate at most places: provosts, deans, or affirmative action officers will distribute to search committees a list of illegal questions to avoid asking job candidates but will do nothing more to prepare the committees. With only this cursory list of *don'ts* in hand, the committee members often feel confused and hamstrung. For instance, when they may want to court a candidate by offering to help find employment for his/her significant other, the committee members remain quiet because they believe broaching that topic is illegal.

What they need to know are acceptable and legal approaches, such as handing out a booklet on the topic or saying to the candidate: "on this campus, we routinely help new faculty hires when their 'significant other' needs assistance in finding meaningful employment. Is that something that would interest you?" A partner's employment has become critical in the hiring process, according to an important national study currently being done by Cathy Trower, a social scientist at Harvard.

It behooves campuses and schools and their search committees to make a gracious overture and then follow up with truly effective assistance (Trower, personal conversation; also see her website).

Some job candidates, of course, would be shy and hesitant about bringing up the topic on their own: this is yet another reason for interviewers to take the lead. Associate Vice Chancellor (and Physics Professor) Bernice Durand at the University of Wisconsin-Madison recommends delivery of the following deft and perfectly legal statement to every finalist: "If information about dual-career assistance interests you, it's right here in this packet of materials I'm giving you. Please let me know of questions you may have before your campus visit ends, or you can email or phone me after your visit is completed" (Durand, conversation).

Failing to coach various evaluation committees—and especially committee chairs--is a *dire* mistake. While the provost or the dean may resort to impressive arguments and rhetorical flourishes as they charge the committees to be fair and careful in their deliberations, such an abstract pep-talk does little good, in my experience. Instead of delivering a pep-talk, these power-holders should insure that evaluation groups engage in thorough preparation as well as in thoughtful review of the cognitive errors and corrupters discussed in this publication. Following review of these, committee members should be given practice sessions (perhaps using the scenarios in Part III of this booklet) to sharpen their skills and alertness.

3. Organizational Dysfunction: No Ground Rules.

Before the search or evaluation commences, the committee should have time to consult and discuss with the department chair, the dean, the hospital director, the technology-transfer officer (or any other relevant officials) the various programmatic needs and opportunities to be considered and decided on before the process goes forward. Because this all-important ground rule is often ignored, committee members in the midst of their work are likely to become confused and enraged with one another: "You're dead wrong. That's not the reason we're trying to fill the vacancy. I never heard and certainly never agreed to such nonsense" or "The dean is simply not going to get a patent law expert. I refuse to go along with him or with the rest of you. That's my position."

Other key issues must be clarified before the committee is activated, including

- how committee members will help one another rise above cognitive shortcuts and errors
- what are the criteria to be used for selection
- what are the *preferred* versus the *required* credentials, experience, and skills being sought
- what discretion will the committee possess if it wishes to bend a requirement in the face of compelling reasons (such as the candidate has not published six law review articles as required but has published five articles and two chapters in two books; or the candidate's book has been accepted for publication but won't be out for eight months).

Also included in preliminary stage of a search should be the construction of the job advertisement and announcement so that these documents constitute an effective, appealing *broad net*—rather than a cut-and-dried narrow net probably used repeatedly in the past. If the committee is rushed, it will likely forget to underscore some attractive new features on the campus, such as: *The college is currently seeking new faculty members who, through their intellectual expertise, teaching, advising, campus and/or community service, demonstrate dedication to the educational benefits of diversity. *The university now has a Dual Career Coordinator to serve the needs of dual-career couples. *The college has begun to actively promote more collaborative work among faculty members and among faculty and students. *For many years, this institute has had a very effective, formal mentoring program for all early-stage members.*

Let's focus quickly on a school's formal mentoring program. If that formal program has demonstrated success in helping early-stagers adjust and become effective teachers, clinicians, legal advocates, scholars, or business innovators, then the existence of that mentoring infrastructure should be underscored in the job announcement. Peg Boyle Single, an expert on mentoring and faculty development, urges that a department's or school's good practices-- already in place to enrich newcomers and early-stagers-- should be *heralded* not ignored. Many prospective job candidates will find these good practices reassuring and appealing (conversation with Single who is Research Associate Professor of Education, University of Vermont).

In addition, do not forget to emphasize *preferred* (as opposed to *required*) skills, experience, and competency in the job announcement. Using the word *preferred* will open the door to equivalent expertise, expertise that often goes unrecognized when departments construct their searches the same old way, year after year (Turner, 17).

In addition, the job announcement wherever possible should be less rigid about the minimum number of years required for a post; often these thresholds were not seriously scrutinized but instead set superficially and allowed to ossify. In short, key ground rules can interrupt business as usual and enhance careful evaluations.

4. Organizational Dysfunction: Absence of Reminders and Monitoring.

Given that cognitive errors and shortcuts are so automatic and deep-seated, there must be reminders to committees about the contaminating power of these errors on their evaluation and decision processes. Why not give each committee member a large index card that lists all the errors, so committee members can handily refresh their memory? Or on the wall of the meeting room, why not hang a banner that lists the errors? Or what about some sort of posted checklist like those often seen in hospitals: *Remember to wash your hands often; confirm the identity of the patient; check for drug allergies; be sure to carefully monitor this and that.*

Why not have the dean check in every two weeks or so with each evaluation committee, to see if perennial errors and bad habits are being avoided? Why not have Equity Advisors (senior faculty leaders who have received special coaching) provide assistance to search committees when they encounter problems? And why not remind important committees that the outside world is concerned about critical issues, such as gender imbalance? In 2004, after media criticism of imbalance, Canadian universities heard "the wake-up call": they nominated and chose a much higher number of women to be Canada Research Chairs ("Women's Gains").

A gentler wake-up call from inside the school can occur when members of powerful committees attend Diversity Dialogues and become more aware of how women and non-immigrant minorities are perennially and unwittingly shortchanged and how cognitive errors can contaminate the

assessments, in fact, of many others. A campus where I consult is seeing very promising results, following a series of six dialogues (which I helped to organize) for its key committees. The campus's search committees, for instance, are reporting confidence that they are no longer merely screening but indeed *searching* and are on guard against cognitive shortcuts and biases.

One of the easiest ways to help a search or tenure review committee stay on track and avoid cognitive quicksand is to include an external "process person" as a member. Serving as a kind of designated driver (who may or may not have a vote), the process person actively monitors the committee's work as it is unfolding. With the committee chair's assistance, the process person helps nudge the committee's deliberations away from irrelevant concerns or cognitive errors and back to careful and judicious gathering and interpreting of evidence. Another approach: the chair can rotate the process-monitoring role to first one internal member (for two weeks or so) and then to others.

There may be some resistance to monitoring, quality-control checks, or having deans and department chairs drop in on evaluation proceedings. A search or tenure review committee may claim that their academic freedom would be violated if their work is scrutinized or made more transparent. This seems to me a misunderstanding of academic freedom. Such freedom doesn't exist to protect subjectivity and lack of accountability for sloppy evaluations and decision-making. Rather, the freedom exists to protect professionals whose political expressions and protests may antagonize power-holders within and without the institution. Academic freedom should protect faculty's rights as active and even outspoken citizens.

5. Organizational Dysfunction: No One Accountable.

The committee chair is seldom expected to update the dean, provost, equity advisors, or diversity council on how the various stages of an ongoing search or evaluation are progressing. Far more disclosure is needed in these processes. Annual job-performance assessments of deans and department chairs seldom include their and their units' evaluation efforts and outcomes (unfortunately many places do not even have performance reviews of their department chairs or program and center directors, a puzzling situation that should be corrected).

But what is promising is a number of campuses and professional schools that are collecting data regarding hiring results by gender and race, and making the information readily available to those involved in hiring, to the campus community, and to state legislators and state auditors who should request the information (O'Rourke). The same request for data should be extended to start-up packages offered and accepted by new hires, in all fields.

6. Organizational Dysfunction: Lack of Debriefing and Systematic Improvement.

Year in and year out, most searches and evaluations go forward without consulting the past experiences and hard-earned wisdom of those who have gone before.

At the present time, only a few schools tap into the wisdom of former search and tenure review chairs and invite these leaders to meet with new search and tenure chairs. And why not make these leaders' caveats and recommendations available in a comprehensive evaluation primer? Within the demystifying primer could be other important items: case studies of actual successful and unsuccessful searches, practice exercises, and a summary of model ground rules that other schools and departments have used to govern evaluations and decision-making.

There could be debriefing of every evaluation committee, in order to add their own "lessons learned" to the primer. Because so little institutional history and wisdom are being recorded at the present time, each committee packs up and sets out on its own—with the likelihood that it will make some predictably amateurish mistakes. Job candidates themselves have insights to share. An associate dean (or perhaps several Equity Advisors) could make it a habit to interview from time to time a number of candidates who turned down the campus's job offers as well as candidates who were not offered jobs.

Another Segue

Having examined bad organizational practices together with individuals' cognitive shortcuts and errors, I want to shift our attention. Can you and I do something constructive about the cognitive errors and the flawed organizational practices? Is there any hope? The answers to both these questions: *yes.*

18

PART II

HOW CAN WE <u>RISE ABOVE</u> COGNITIVE ERRORS AS WELL AS <u>REMEDY</u> DYSFUNCTIONAL PRACTICES THAT INTENSIFY THE ERRORS?

1. Constant Self-Correction by Individuals and Committees

As individuals, you and I must have the clear intention to rise above the fifteen cognitive errors and shortcuts, and we must devote real concentration to the task. It's not enough to say "well, I can't imagine how I could improve my own evaluation and thinking processes. If my processes are so bad, how could I have gotten to be a senior supervisor?" Such a stance must be set aside. To move from preconscious, intuitive, simple thinking to conscious thinking and deliberate reasoning requires sharp and daily attention. But such attention can indeed move you and me to higher ground, according to dozens of cognitive scientists. Department chairs and other high-level administrators must appreciate how much work, over time, will be necessary if those involved in searches and reviews are to reach and remain on the higher plane.

2. Coaching, Preparation, and Reminders (such as Index Cards).

A few campuses are paying more than lip service to better preparation of their faculty. The University of Washington has constructed its "Toolkit for Faculty Recruitment" and the University of Wisconsin its "Reviewing Applicants" brochure. Both of these are *exemplary* and available at the campuses' websites, more specifically under descriptions of their National Science Foundation ADVANCE

programs on those two campuses, programs dedicated to greater gender equity.

My own naming and then illustrating of fifteen cognitive errors should also prove helpful for faculty and administrators (at least I hope so). Using this publication and others as the focus of training or coaching sessions would be sensible. But individuals must also be constantly *reminded* to hold on to their resolve and rise above bad cognitive habits. A Nobel Laureate behavioral economist puts it this way: you have to receive "stronger cues for relevant rules" in order to improve decision-making and wean yourself from simple-minded, automatic thinking (Kahneman, p. 711; also see Sturm and Guinier). Those stronger cues could appropriately come from a supervisor, dean, chair, provost, or cadre of Equity Advisors.

As I mentioned earlier, why not give every member of every search or evaluation committee a large *index card* (to refer to every time they meet) that lists the typical errors and biases to avoid? Without a tickler system, you and I can easily fall into simple patterns: we will far more easily notice and file into our memory any behavior and information that is *compatible* with our stereotypes and prior framing. We will less automatically notice and file in our memory any behavior and information that go against the grain of these stereotypes and our prior framing (Biernat, Kahneman).

Workshops, of course, can serve as reminders. Six months after running one on a New England campus, I received this email from an attendee: "In any fast-paced academic setting (like ours and many others), I think we sometimes plow through applicants' materials too quickly. But as a result of your workshop, I found myself being more thoughtful and mindful as I was reviewing candidates' files this time around" (personal communication). But experience prompts me to say that this faculty member, like all others, will surely need constant reminders, cues, and practice in order to maintain that mindfulness. We all do.

Committee chairs, without a doubt, deserve their own tailor-made coaching sessions: they must understand and be able to deal with the typical dynamics of committee work, to give light-handed but firm feedback to members, and know how to short-circuit predictable problems, such as one member becoming *monopolizer-for-the-day*; another resorting to sarcasm to put down others' points; another becoming passive, disengaged, and wedded to their text messaging (Whetten and Cameron, pp. 467-8). New techniques should be tried, such as periodically asking members to email their reactions about candidates to the chair, for the purpose of stimulating deeper reflection and breaking up a dominant member's filibuster or other verbal hold on the process.

Newly established search committees should have the chance to learn from more experienced search chairs (from outside and inside the home campus). I applaud the Universities of Michigan and California-Irvine and their ADVANCE-NSF programs for forming cadres of Equity Advisors (tenured senior faculty and former search chairs) who regularly meet with new search committees: to share insights and caveats, to help solve problems that occur during the search process, and especially to outline proven ways to identify and hire more women and minorities.

Having senior faculty coach other faculty is a wise approach, and one that I encourage during my consulting work with campuses and schools. When a dean or provost in a heavy-handed manner hands down an ultimatum and strict directives from "on high" regarding how a search or other evaluation should be conducted, the rebellion of faculty will *not* be far behind. Far better, in my view, is to have the dean, provost, and outside consultants coach important committees on perennial errors to avoid and, at the same time, coach a dozen or so senior faculty leaders from across the campus so they can become the Equity Advisors to their colleagues in years to come. This education and prompting takes more time but delivers more sticking power.

3. Ground Rules and Preparation for the Evaluation Process

Prior to the start of the evaluation, the committee chair could profitably take an hour and ask each member to name the three *most troublesome* problems they have experienced in past committee work. When the problems are set out on the table, then it will be clear why ground rules must be developed that will prevent the repetition of these vexing problems in the current process (personal conversation with management and leadership expert Professor Joan Tonn).

Secondly, the chair (together with a dean perhaps) might then lead members through a checklist found within the campus's or division's policies and personnel handbooks and also through a disclosure of "lessons learned," compliments of previous committees. The checklist for a faculty search, for instance, would predictably advise members to consider and discuss:

- the strengths and weaknesses of the hiring department and its likely needs in the short and long-term
- the more specific programmatic needs (including the maximizing of the educational benefits of diversity) that the new hire would serve
- the steps and stages of the search process

- how pro-active outreach and "head-hunting" will be specifically done (as opposed to wholesale screening out of candidates who respond to an ad)
- how quality control within the process will be guaranteed
- how tasks will be divided so that the committee's work is done in a thorough manner
- how both phone and face-to-face interviews will be conducted
- how the results of each stage of the process will be recorded
- how and from whom the committee, will seek extra help with problem-solving, during its deliberations.

Once a number of ground rules have been agreed upon, the committee chair and the dean can ask if any other guidelines should be considered and adopted. Note: A number of campuses like Michigan State University have posted to their websites valuable and time-saving checklists and ground rules for search, tenure/promotion review, and other committees to use.

Probably the most important ground rule, in my view, is insisting on *evidence rather than opinions* as the evaluation goes forward. The chair and the designated process person (see below) should have the responsibility of keeping the committee on track with its own assessment criteria and, above all, insisting that members "show us the evidence that warrants your statement or conclusion." In particular, when a candidate is close to being removed from the running, it is essential that those members indicating a "thumbs down" should give ample details and evidence--as opposed to offering superficial rankings (such as, *he's a weak number 10 in my view*) to justify their pending decision. If sufficient evidence is not forthcoming, then the ground rule would require that the candidate be restored to the active pool under consideration.

4. Diverse Committee; Process Monitor
The composition of the evaluation committee is important. Whenever possible, there should be a diversity of backgrounds among the members, as mentioned earlier. This internal diversity usually results in a greater diversity of candidates and applicants being identified and given serious attention. In addition, organizational experts recommend a diversity of backgrounds and perspectives within a decision-making unit in order to mitigate the pressures and tunnel vision of "group-think" that occurs with a homogeneous committee (Nelson & Quick).

Equally important is for an evaluation committee to scrutinize the stages of its own work in order to avoid unintentional contaminants and cutting of corners. An effective way to do this: share the role of "process monitor." For two weeks, have one member of the committee assume the monitoring of all aspects of the evaluation process and assist the chair in moving members away from seeming errors. Then rotate the process role to another member for the next two weeks and so on. If an outside process monitor is brought in (from another department, for instance), then usually that person is not granted a vote in the deliberations. The reason? To safeguard the integrity of the process and prevent the reality or the appearance that the external process expert is lobbying for a favorite person or for a specific decision. This personnel safeguard has worked well in the several management schools.

Who chooses the external process person? I suggest that both the dean and the department chair put their heads together and jointly appoint a senior, respected colleague as the process monitor. This role necessitates knowledge and experience of relevant procedures and policies as well as considerable interpersonal skills (personal conversation with Joan Tonn, organizational management expert). That is why the process person should be carefully chosen, generously coached, and then appointed to the committee. A small department will probably have to recruit a process person from another department. Once a process person has gained experience, then she or he can assist with the coaching of other monitors for future evaluations.

Note that a temporary "devil's advocate" can be helpful in interrupting group momentum and complacency (Cognitive Error #15 discussed above). The advocate surfaces potential pitfalls and shortcomings for decisions seemingly favored by a majority of members. In this way, the rigor of the committee debate can be reactivated. The committee chair should assign the critic's role from time to time and *rotate* it among the members (Nelson and Quick, p. 344; also Ancona *et al*).

5. Use a Matrix for Keeping on Track.
Some schools have their evaluation committees set up a visual matrix of the six to twelve or so categories of skills, abilities, and qualifications that are desired or required in the successful job, tenure, or grant applicant. The chair and the process person can then ask members for *evidence* about candidates, one by one--evidence that is directly related to these concrete, visual categories in the matrix. Members who slide off into tangents, irrelevant considerations, and free-wheeling opinions can be brought back on board, with this visual cue. A number of departments at New Mexico State University employ such a matrix (personal conversation with Agronomy and Horticulture Professor Mary O'Connell). The beauty of the matrix is that it can guide

the committee's deliberations and help to keep members focused.

6. Slow Down Evaluations; Don't Overload; Provide Assistance.
Committee members must have the time to anticipate and discuss the tasks ahead of them and decide how they will help one another avoid the cognitive errors I've named. Administrators should not ask nor allow the committee to immediately jump into reviewing applications.

What else can administrators do? Assign extra secretarial or other administrative support. Excuse evaluation members from other less important committee assignments that take up their time. Experiment with ways to increase the "yield" achieved by the search: perhaps hire a "head-hunter" consultant; perhaps provide money so that a faculty member in a department can do year-round recruitment and cultivation of possible job candidates and bring these to the attention of the official search committee. A former chair of psychology at the University of Michigan was "superb" at the task of identifying promising graduate students and cultivating their interest in joining his department, according to Ted Marchese, former vice president at the American Association of Higher Education (personal conversation). Through such enthusiastic cultivation, a department can be assured of a steady stream of candidates who already have positive rapport with the department.

Once the search or evaluation committees are given more time and support, then administrators should set high expectations that the committees will execute vigorous "head-hunting" outreach, will encourage applications from qualified people who have not yet applied, and will devote more attention and self-correction to their review tasks. Finally, administrators should stand ready to provide committees with counseling, brainstorming assistance, and perhaps extra money if the committees are confronted with snags or special circumstances (such as, an insufficient number of applicants; the desire to bring in five finalists to interview rather than three, due to opportunities that have just developed; the desire for additional external letters for the tenure candidate; and so on).

7. Incorporate Accountability into Evaluation Processes.

Members of the evaluation committee should be held accountable. This means you as a member should monitor yourself, of course. But primarily this means that appropriate others—such as an official with standing from the dean's office--should at times watch and take note of how well you and the search or evaluation committee are doing at rising above typical errors. At a small liberal arts campus I work with, the vice provost makes it a habit to drop in (unannounced) at one time or another on each faculty search committee. This administrator tells me that his mere presence "tones up" the proceedings, without his uttering a word or lifting an eyebrow. In addition, the committee chair and the process person should meet regularly with the department chair and/or dean, to give updates and seek advice when needed.

As part of their own annual job-performance appraisal, deans and department chairs should be assessed on how well they prepare and monitor evaluation committees under their jurisdiction. A number of campuses and professional schools are in the process of setting up such assessment protocols.

The peer-review system itself, in science and all other fields, must become more transparent and fair. Studies of the peer-

review process at a number of scientific research councils in Europe have been recently launched, in response to the shocking findings of contaminants within the Swedish Research Council's evaluation processes for awarding post-doctoral grants. (Recall that Sweden prides itself on its devotion to social equality.) *Nature*, the highly influential journal that published the Swedish findings, underscored that the results "severely undermine the credibility of the peer-review system, not just in Sweden but elsewhere in the world" (Payne, quoted in the electronic magazine of the European Life Scientist Organization).

Nature editors and other science leaders have called for a scientific evaluation of the evaluation processes used within peer-review, in order to root out contaminants such as *bias* (extra points added) that benefit male applicants; *prejudice* (points subtracted) that harms female applicants; and the *affiliation bonus* (a kind of cloning bonus) tacitly awarded to an applicant connected with someone who recuses himself on the peer-review committee (Wenneras and Wold, "Nepotism and Sexism"). Further, a variety of leaders are calling for regular publishing of statistics about the advancement of women, men, and various ethnic groups in order to detect patterns of inequity. Those leaders also insist that more light be directed into all corners of peer-review and its conventions, assumptions, and protocols.

8. Use Simulations and Other Unconventional Approaches in Interviews to Gain a Fuller Picture of Applicants

Members of search and other evaluation committees should be alert to their often unwitting preference to seek conventional, standard information from the candidates or colleagues being scrutinized. And beware the searching for evidence and details that confirm one's own preconceptions and first impressions. To actually see and appreciate an *unexpected attribute* in an applicant will require more-than-usual evidence for the judge (you or I). For instance, financial competence in a *woman* candidate for a finance post would be a conventionally unexpected trait. So be sure to gather abundant details that such an attribute does exist—some on the committee will at times need abundant evidence to see and then willingly give serious consideration.

As a safeguard, give candidates from disfavored groups ample time and opportunity to demonstrate that they do indeed possess the unexpected, positive attributes, whatever they are. To do this, organizations must *lengthen interviews*. Using the standard allotted time usually is usually not long enough for some faculty and administrators to overcome their unease and discomfort with non-majority candidates and draw out and process non-stereotypical information about them. Several of the scholars I have mentioned are adamant about this. So my overall recommendation is this: lengthen the interviews for *all* final job candidates or fellowship and grant applicants. Gathering more details and evidence will enable the evaluators to circumvent stereotypical assumptions about one person being, for instance, *obviously* competent and a "good fit" while another is obviously incompetent and a "bad fit."

Borrowing a technique from corporate hiring, I also recommend that applicants and candidates be given the same job *simulation* (or mini case study) that requires them to analyze a teaching or research problem, for instance, and then outline several ways to resolve it. Seeing different candidates' approaches and thought processes can bring invaluable information to the table. Corporations have found simulations effective in getting beyond interviewees' canned speeches and conventional answers.

9. Avoid Numerical Rankings.
When the finalists are selected, all of them in this last stage should be *acceptable to hire.* Don't rank (I repeat: don't rank) finalists in a faculty or staff search--such as, "John is our first choice; Mary our second; Tomas our third. We really hope we get our first choice." I issue this caveat advisedly.

Reducing complex information to a single number is a very dangerous shortcut. Instead, the search or selection committee should write up summaries of each finalist's strengths, weaknesses, promise, and likely contributions to students, patients, clients, department, and campus. Cite an abundance of evidence, not opinions, in those written summaries. Additionally, make a point to refer often to the components of the job description or to the matrix discussed above. Such an *evidence-based written exercise* is itself clarifying: it will reveal what cognitive approaches are being used and it will insure more detailed and rigorous deliberations in this final stage of the search process.

Ranking creates problems. Remember that many surprises and detours can ensue between the point when the finalists are chosen and when one of them actually signs the contract. Recall how often a finalist will accept another school's offer, withdraw for no stated reason, turn away because their significant other cannot find meaningful employment, or walk away because they and the hiring department and/or dean cannot get to "yes" on the terms of employment.

Given these predictable surprises and complex developments, it is wise to maintain all finalists in the *active-hiring* pool. Thirdly, ranking final candidates can and often does backfire. When a hiring department and dean are left with someone who has not been deemed "number one" (because of the complexities mentioned above), then many involved in the search process will feel let down. Needless to say, intense demoralization also awaits the *new hire* when they discover they themselves were *not* placed at the top of the list. In short, bad feelings can be easily generated by the bad practice of ranking. I recommend avoidance of ranking, rating, and lazy reliance on such numbers.

10. Avoid Solo Situations; Include Several Minorities in the Pool of Finalists.

In a job search or in a peer-review of grant applications, include two or more women and non-immigrant minorities in the finalists' pool, if at all possible. Having several members from negatively stereotyped groups in the pool (as well as graduates of less prestigious programs) makes it easier for committee members to see differences between these candidates and to get beyond superficial and stereotypical responses and gut-feelings (Valian). In other words, having two or more will probably prevent members from seeing the solo candidate (the token) as the embodiment of the group stereotype, with no distinguishing individual traits. But let me underscore this caveat: guard against the notion that the only thing required is to have a woman, a minority, and a graduate from a less prestigious campus in the group of finalists. Something is wrong if only those from the same old sources ever get hired.

11. Continuous Practice.

Continuous practice is indispensable for recognizing and rising above bad cognitive habits. For example, individuals, councils of deans, evaluation committees, presidents' cabinets, boards of trustees, and entire academic departments could analyze and discuss Scenarios in Part III of this

publication. I frequently compose and use scenarios and problem-based exercises in my consulting with campuses, professional schools, government labs, and so on.

Accomplished search and/or tenure committee chairs from other campuses can be brought in to coach and practice newly formed committees. In addition, consult and share with others the on-line preparatory materials and tutorials for search committees (see the University of Virginia's website) as well as for tenure and promotion committees (see Georgia Tech's website).

Finally, consider offering practice to evaluators in the form of *dramatized* mini case studies. Within the University of Michigan's Center for Research on Learning and Teaching is a highly acclaimed interactive theatre program. Using a troupe of local professional and student actors directed by Jeffrey Steiger, this program dramatizes sketches about dysfunctional faculty search processes, tenure reviews, and classroom approaches. A trained facilitator guides the audience's discussion of the sketch. Relatedly, leadership developers at MIT's Sloan School of Management, the University of Florida, and Allegheny College employ videotaped sketches and scenarios to prepare important committees as well as brand-new administrators.

12. Personal Relationships to Diminish Social Distance.

Starting this week, you as an individual could resolve to deliberately develop friendly and personal relationships with several members of groups often the target of negative stereotypes. Why? You need to store up non-stereotypical experiences to draw on. Pinker has shown that positive first-hand encounters and personal experiences can diminish the powerful and automatic hold on us of negative stereotypes (also see www.implicit.harvard.edu).

Citing a number of national studies, Professor Caroline Turner at Arizona State University concurs: "the development of sustained, personal relationships can help to dispel racial myths and stereotypes." Turner, together with other analysts, calls on campuses themselves to sponsor supervised activities and conversations where the social distance between members of different racial/ethnic groups can be diminished and community can be built (p. 17). I applaud those campuses that are sponsoring Sustained Diversity Dialogues for their students, faculty, staff, and trustees.

13. Courage and Resolve from Leaders to Insist: "Show Me the Evidence."
In undertaking self-correction in public and private, you and I are admitting that we must rise above some sloppy thinking and bad habits. This could be a hard admission.

Non-offensively alerting our colleagues to their own employment of one or another cognitive error or shortcut—this too will be a new task requiring courage and finesse. Easy, bad habits will have to give way. An all-too-familiar scenario occurs when an extremely opinionated committee member, through endless repetition, wears down his or her colleagues to the end-point of acquiescence. Neither opinions nor their repetition nor the acquiescence of the exhausted can be tolerated in the new evaluation process. Instead, "show me the evidence" must become the mantra within evaluation processes in order to dispel superficial decision-making and to remain steadily on a higher cognitive level.

Provosts, deans, and department chairs must be ready to defend the new ways of conducting evaluations. In fact, these power-holders should lead the way through their own example of self-correction and their own insistence on "show me the *evidence*."

14. Constant Attention to Improvement; Debriefing.
Debriefings of evaluation processes (similar to those done after hospital surgeries) are worth the investment. Incremental improvements in evaluation processes should be the goal. For instance,

- Primers can be written to share lessons learned from earlier evaluations.
- Senior Equity Advisors can be activated, to offer on-going guidance and problem-solving assistance to a variety of gate-keeping committees.
- A checklist of ground rules, together with important checks-and-balances, can prevent careless or rushed proceedings and decisions.
- Small experiments can reveal better ways to coach and refresh committee chairs and process monitors.

Conclusion
We can stop doing evaluations in the same old, unexamined, and contaminated way.

Being able to name and then rise above common cognitive errors and shortcuts can become a new personal habit for us.

Effective checks-and-balances, skills-development workshops, task-oriented reminders, clear protocols, and detailed checklists can be adopted by departments, divisions, and organizations.

And day in and day out, we can commit ourselves to constant self-correction and practice so that higher-order thinking remains within our grasp.

PART III

SCENARIOS FOR ANALYSIS AND PRACTICE

The following five scenarios (or mini-case studies) are offered to prompt reflection and problem-solving, not only in formal meetings but also in informal conversations among faculty, administrators, and staff. The cognitive errors and organizational dysfunctions presented in the scenarios are only slightly exaggerated—I have encountered all of them and on a regular basis. Scenarios prove to important problem-based vehicles for engaging colleagues in thoughtful analysis of their school's and department's disorders and in collectively mulling over possible remedies. Scenarios are especially helpful to feature in sessions and retreats for search, tenure, and selection committees and their chairs; for deans; faculty senates; department heads; equity advisors; staff supervisors; trustees; and indeed entire departments and schools.

As you read each scenario, ask yourself:

- What's going wrong here? Going right?
- What cognitive errors and shortcuts are being made by individuals in the scenario?
- What dysfunctions at the organizational level are being illustrated?
- If you were chair of the committee in the scenario, what would you do to replace bad practices with good ones? How would you propose to do that? What caveats should be heeded?
- If you were the dean or provost, what would you do to encourage good practices? How would you propose to do that? What caveats should be heeded?

DISCUSSION SCENARIO #1:
Medical School Committee's Review of a Promotion and Tenure Case

Professor A: Three of these outside letters mention that Shirley is a 'delightful' person with a great deal of 'tact' and 'cordiality.' I think that's *code* and the authors are trying to tell us that she's a lightweight. That fits with my first impression of her.

Professor B: Listen, I'd like to call those authors and insist they give us more details about Shirley's intellectual achievements and less about her personality. But I guess we could easily irritate those three writers, couldn't we? And they could take out their annoyance on our candidate. She could easily become a sitting, defenseless duck.

Professor A: Well, how about if we ask Shirley to give us the names of three or four more external experts who can address the rigor and importance of her scholarly achievements to date. Assuming, of course, that she has some.

Review Committee Chair: Yes, that makes sense. I personally think that we're seeing unintentional gender bias in these three letters in front of us. I'll think we'll also have to be on guard with any other letters that come in to us.

Professor B: Hey, it just occurred to me that maybe the outside letters for our male tenure candidates have been maybe biased the other way. You know, maybe the authors have glossed

27

over weaknesses and just emphasized strengths of the male candidates. How in the world will we know if they got the benefit of the doubt?

Chair: Well, I think we can remind ourselves to look for abundant evidence before we come to decisions about candidates under review. We shouldn't accept any outsider's blanket generalization. We should be looking for real evidence.

Professor A: Here's another odd situation about Shirley. Her department's tenure review committee, by 5 to 1, recommends Shirley for tenure and promotion but points out that she is *always* trying to set limits so that her work commitments don't eat into her family commitments. She's become quite famous for her persistence, hasn't she? What do we make of that? I myself think this means she's not dependable as a team player. Did anyone else pick up that implication? Anyone heard complaints from colleagues working with Shirley? Does she let people down?

Professor B: No, I've heard comments about her fierce concentration and I've heard praise that she always gets the job done---very well. By the way, I know for a fact that two of the four male candidates for tenure we reviewed last week also routinely protest their departments' insensitivity to their family obligations. But I saw little—no, I saw *no*—references to this fact in their departments' summary documents.

Chair: Well, anyway, this is an outside fact that didn't appear in the candidates' official dossiers. Anyone know if we can factor this in to our deliberations? I really don't know.

Professor B: Well, for sure we can see in the file that Shirley has done an overload of service. No wonder she complains and protests. Look at the number of committees she's served on. This is ridiculous. Why didn't her department chair protect her from much of this burden? I do think her overload is relevant for our deliberations. The expectations put on her were way beyond what any of us, as a team player, would be expected to do.

Professor A: Why doesn't Shirley just learn to say **no** to committee assignments?

Professor B: Hey, think about it. What junior faculty member is going to buck the all-powerful chair or the dean? It's the job of the department chair and especially her mentors to exercise some authority and prevent such an overload.

Chair: Hold on. We're supposed to be judging no one except *Shirley*. Though honestly, I think tenure candidates who've had lazy chairs or a lot of turnover of chairs are really getting the short end of the stick. I do think Shirley should get a few extra points for this committee service, regrettable though it was for a junior colleague to have such a load.

Professor A: Are you saying that we should add a few points to our evaluation of Shirley— especially given that her research record seems to need some bolstering? Let's talk about Shirley's publications. Why in the world would her departmental review committee not downgrade her in view of this important fact: almost all her articles deal with how medical diagnoses can be biased against members of minority groups. Looks like another example of her never-stop persistence, to me.

Professor B: Gee, I think we have to look to the quality of the work. Did you actually *read* some of her articles? They're rigorous and impressive. Shirley's scholarship matches up, in quantity and quality, with the average we've used and accepted in the recent past. She's not above that standard but she's not below it, either.

Professor A: Wait a minute. I think Shirley's publications record is also substandard next to the high expectation we should have for *this* year. Raising our standard is the only way to keep enhancing and ratcheting up the reputation of our departments. It's always a moving target, always. That's just a fact of life. We should always be pushing the envelope on what we accept as the 'best and brightest.' That's just a given, though we never talk about it much.

Chair: Hold on, hold on. We must also be sure that we're not raising the bar because Shirley is the first and only non-immigrant minority in her department and one of only twelve throughout the entire school! When someone is associated with a negative stereotype (like Shirley who's African American), then we have to be very careful that we're not raising the bar because we feel uneasy with her qualifications and achievements.

Professor B: I think our job here is to grant tenure to a colleague who is average or above average for our departments and to deny tenure to someone below average for our departments. Remember, please, that being solid and average is a perfectly respectable place to be and a place where *most all* of us *live*. Average certainly means productive and valuable—it does not mean mediocre. To tell you the truth, all this talk about insisting on the 'best and brightest' makes me uncomfortable. I think it's code for something.

Professor A: Why are you so uncomfortable? You've lost me.

Professor B: Seeking only the best and only the brightest—I know that's what many in medical schools and elsewhere think they're supposed to do. But when evaluators say they want to do that, they almost always end up making quick decisions and they end up underestimating and mismeasuring really solid people—people who would make exceptional contributions to our departments, our students, and medical care and discovery. So what I suggest is that we start using the job-criteria matrix we all agreed on, so that we can keep our evaluation in the here and now. I'm uncomfortable with our evaluation moving to some castle in the sky where we think the best and brightest are found.

Professor A: I have absolutely no idea what you're driving at. If you uneasy about evaluations and all, then why did you agree to be on this review committee?

Chair: Hold on. Hold on. Let me shift the subject. Do you think we should take into account that Shirley has been the 'token' or the 'solo' in her department? Being the one and only non-immigrant, under-represented minority over there can't be easy. I'm glad to know that her department is poised to bring in three new hires, two of whom are non-immigrant minorities. But think about it, for her entire career in her department, Shirley has been in a solo position. I don't envy her. Any organizational behavior expert will tell you that solos and pioneers (unlike me and you) have plenty of extra complexities to deal with.

Professor A: Hey, I'm beginning to feel like I'm in a counseling group. We have to measure Shirley the way we do everyone else. And that means our standards go up every year. Maybe she could have made tenure last year but it's *tougher* this year. That's what it means to be a meritocracy: lots of people get the short end of the stick.   END.

DISCUSSION SCENARIO #2:
The Early Stage of a Faculty Search in Engineering

Professor A: I really resent that the trustees are pressuring the university to look more diligently for U.S. minority candidates. Our department, for one, is operated as a meritocracy. Using tough standards for everyone, we objectively choose *only* the best. I absolutely refuse to lower our standards in order to satisfy anyone else! There, that's my position.

Committee Chair: Hey, saying that we are a meritocracy doesn't make us one. How do you explain that almost all our colleagues have degrees from MIT or Cal Tech—and are European-American or Asian-Indian men to boot? Looks like a monopoly to someone on the outside, I'd say, rather than a meritocracy. And, just for the record, the dean said that we should "hire new faculty who satisfy the department's standards and programmatic needs." I wrote down those words verbatim. I didn't hear any implication from him that we should lower our standards.

Professor A: Oh, fine. Fine. But I can guarantee it's going to be difficult if not impossible to identify some qualified minority candidates, unless we go way outside our national borders. You know what I mean. Here's my caveat: I don't think we should call or invite anyone to apply. Let them read our ad like everyone else. I think the law is clear that we can't reach out in any special way to any special population.

Professor B: I don't agree. We do special outreach all the time, and it's not illegal. For instance, every year some of us call around to our colleagues to see whom they recommend as outstanding prospects for us. And several times in the past, remember, we've approached senior faculty at other campuses and asked them to apply when we had a serious vacuum in some subspecialty or a promising opportunity in a multidisciplinary enterprise. Besides, some minority folks won't consider us, I'm positive, unless we make the first move. We don't exactly have a stellar reputation for hiring and retaining minorities, you know. So I say we should become more pro-active in our recruiting, as the dean urged. But notice that the dean didn't give us any extra administrative support or—heaven forbid—a little more money. So how are we going to pull off this pro-active stuff?

Professor A: Here's what I recommend to save time: let's find candidates who most resemble our dearly departed colleague, Tim. It's unbelievable to me that he's been gone almost two years. His death has left a void in the department. Our search should be easy because we know the kind of researcher, colleague, and supervisor of students we're looking for.

Professor B: Listen, I myself have already called a few of my buddies across the country. I've identified four strong candidates for us from underrepresented minority groups. Can I summarize their qualifications and show you their C.V.s?

Professor A: Not so fast. Isn't it illegal to do that? Shouldn't their CVs be put in the pile now before us?

Chair: Well, we're certainly going to scrutinize these four the same way we do all the other candidates. All that's being said is that these four probably wouldn't have applied to us. If we see some promise in one or more of them, we can *invite* them to apply and to be evaluated just like everyone else. Is it a deal? Whether they do apply or not is their business.

Professor A: Well, it feels odd. But, I guess we've done some of this in the past when we called our old friends or mentors at Yale or Stanford or wherever and asked them to name some outstanding grad students or post-docs we might hire. That old method certainly took less time than wading through all these C.V.s staring at us. But still, we can pretty quickly figure out who's our first choice. That's always easy for me.

Chair: Hold on. Hold on. Before we even look at these C.V.s and start our evaluation process, I want us to construct and agree on some ground rules to govern the work of our committee. Allow me, please, to give each of you a list of fifteen rules that Michigan's search committees have started to use. The dean gave me this list. Let's look at these rules. Then let's discuss them, one by one, and either adopt, change, or reject each one. And you can bring up some rules of your own invention, too. You probably have some in mind, since both of you are veterans on the faculty search circuit. So let's begin. Okay?

Professor A: Sure, sure. Let's go one by one. But you said we'd end our meeting in 30 minutes, remember? I really don't have time for all this. You and the dean are just making things far too complex.   END.

DISCUSSION SCENARIO #3:
A Community College Search Committee Prepares to Interview Job Candidates

Professor A: I've been wrestling with the fact that two of our five candidates coming in for interviews have doctoral degrees from Northwest universities. We've never ventured that far afield, have we? That makes me a bit uneasy.

Committee Chair: Well, we didn't specify any special location for the doctoral universities when we were deciding on ground rules. We certainly can't make up a geography rule now.

Professor A: Okay, fine. Listen, I'll volunteer to call both candidates from the Northwest and make sure they realize what it's like to live and work in the South. And, you know, I should make sure they're genuinely interested in our college and seem serious enough for tenure-track.

Chair: No thanks. No. It's my responsibility to talk with any candidates over the phone. That's one of the ground rules, remember? The dean gave me a course release so that I could devote adequate time to chairing this committee and to covering all bases. That's what I intend to do.

Professor A: Well, okay. I'll volunteer to pick up these two candidates at the airport and bring them to the campus. I can do that, can't I?

Chair: No thanks. I want all candidates we interview to take a taxi from the airport to the campus, and back again.

Professor B: Why in the world would you want such an impersonal procedure? I thought we agreed to gather much more info and evidence during this search than we ever have before.

Chair: Yes, but under conditions where all of us are involved and engaged. Remember when I said it's been unfair in the past for some finalists to get the red-carpet treatment while others didn't. Some have received inside information in one way or another, and some have not.

Professor A: Well, I really don't see how my driving a candidate around could 'contaminate' our proceedings. But whatever. It was a ground rule we agreed to, I guess. But I begin to wonder if we're converting this search into an obsessive-compulsive exercise in futility. Just kidding….

Chair: Of course.

Professor B: I would like to move that we rank the finalists before they get here for their interviews and job talks. Knowing the line-up would help us do our job faster, wouldn't it?

Chair: No. Indeed it m   Every candidate's campus visit will provide us new information and insigh   e.

Professor A: Listen,   d. But really, I have all the evidence I need, right

Professor B: Haven'

Chair: Listen, I wan   prevent inadvertent favoritism and inadvertent pro   idates but not to others. Let's remember that all ca   e Equity Advisors appointed by the dean. I don't   hind-the-scenes coaching while another says he trie   tain answers about departmental policies from anyo   ver the past ten years, you know.

Professor A: Nov   are making you *nervous*. Whose idea was it, anyw   all corners of the campus become the equity police and iora

Chair: I'm not nervous. But I do want our committee be deliberate and careful in its interviews and decision-making.

Professor A: Look, the Equity Advisors do not have the right to violate my or your academic freedom. As members of this committee, we do not have to answer to them or to anyone else.

Chair: Oh yes, we do. Searches can't be cavalierly run, as they usually were in the past. That's for sure.

Professor A: Oh, my gosh. Don't tell me that 'cavalier' is now a dirty word. Political correctness is taking over this entire campus!   END.

DISCUSSION SCENARIO #4:
Search for a New Director of Finance

The search committee below is seeking to hire a director of finance for a large comprehensive university on the West Coast. The three committee members include: the director of campus facilities; the dean of the faculty (who is chairing this committee); and a business leader.

Member A: Well, I think Tom is the strongest candidate, by far. His M.B.A. from Harvard is all we need to know. He's got to be sound; he's just that type of guy. That's my judgment. I don't need any more evidence. He's number one with me.

Committee Chair: I don't think we can move that fast. We have four people coming in for face-to-face interviews. I'd like to hope that we'll gather new information about them and have time to sift through their strengths, weaknesses, and likely meeting of our needs for this position.

Member A: Yes, yes, of course. All of you gather as much info as you like. I have no problem with that. It's just that I don't have much time right now. Oh, another reason that Tom seems like the top candidate is that he reminds me so much of Mervin. Man, how this campus misses that guy! Now there was a finance director to hold up as the gold standard. Getting someone very much like Mervin would certainly be a plus for us.

Chair: Look, I'd like for us to review what additional info we want to gather about each of the candidates coming in. While I had wanted to figure out some ground rules before we started all this and also construct a job-criteria matrix to put up on the wall, none of this happened. So let's just move on. Can we talk about Ricardo? He has the right kind of experience, having been associate director of finance at Michigan State. His letters of recommendation are superb. Does anyone want to call up the references and get more details?

Member A: Well, I have trouble giving much credence to those letters. None of Ricardo's letters was written by people whom I know or have ever heard of. I can't put much stock in them, to tell you the truth. And to boot, did you notice that one of his letters of support had two grammatical errors in it? Come on, now. That tells you something.

Member B: You've got to be kidding! Can we get back to Ricardo himself. I'd like to make sure that our interview takes at least two hours. I want us to get to know him. Given that we've never had a minority candidate before, I think we'd better go slow and give this candidate plenty of time to prove his qualifications. And it'll take us some time to really feel comfortable with him, I would bet. Besides, some of us---who will go unnamed--- might have some negative stereotypes about Puerto Rican Americans and other minorities in leadership roles to work through.

Member A: Wait a minute. Wait a minute. Why in the world should we give Ricardo such an advantage? Interviewing him for two hours! Be serious! We'd gather more info than we could ever use. Seems like a colossal waste of time to me. And I for one don't have a minute to waste this semester. I say we stick with the program: every candidate gets a 45-minute interview; we'll use our standard questions. Every candidate gives a 60-minute job talk and then meets with deans, staff, and the usual suspects. These procedures have never failed us in the past, have they?

Member B: Well, maybe they have. Basically, I don't think an hour is enough time for *any* candidate, but especially for a non-traditional one like Ricardo. I'd like to see if we can have the candidates analyze a simulation (you know, a short case study) and tell us how they'd deal with the problems in it. For sure, we'd need two hours for that. Maybe we can revisit this time question later.

Member A: May I ask why you're so eager to give Ricardo some extra breaks. Look, we're supposed to be looking for the very best person for the position. I really could care less if the person we hire is black, purple, green, polka-dot, male, female, or whatever. I know that I am gender-blind and color-blind. All I care about is *excellence.* And we'll know it when we see it. Do you want to know *one* of my hesitations about Ricardo? His M.B.A. is from a second-tier school. I'd really feel better about him if he had a degree from Stanford or Harvard. And I think we should get a few more letters of reference from him. Just to be cautious, you know.

Member B: Cautious about what? Why in the world would you want extra letters about Ricardo but not about the three European-American male candidates? Is it because Ricardo doesn't fulfill our expectation of what a finance director should look like? Why such uneasiness?

Member A: Well, I don't like to admit this. But, okay, I'm a bit uneasy about Ricardo because I'm not sure how the staff working with him would like it. You know, answering to him as the *boss*. We could really be asking for trouble.

Chair: Well, allow me to remind you that the director now leaving in a huff created a multitude of personnel problems, coming and going. That guy was impossible to work with. A sheer autocrat. So we have to be on guard against such personality traits and work habits in all our candidates. If anything, Ricardo seems more mature and seasoned than the other candidates.

Member A: Well, here's another hesitation I have. Ricardo is single, right? Do you thing he's gay? That's okay with me, but I don't think he'd be comfortable in our town. It's so family-oriented and all. We should consider Ricardo's happiness. I just don't think he's a good fit.

Chair: Listen, why don't we take ten minutes to decompress and get some coffee?   END.

DISCUSSION SCENARIO #5:
Final Stage of a Faculty Search Process at a Midwest Law School

Professor A: Well, I've been saying this for the past two weeks: Walter has got to be 'number one' for all of us. I can't see it any other way. Basically we've wasted hundreds of hours scrutinizing other candidates who can't hold a candle to him.

Committee Chair: You haven't really ever explained in detail why Walter is so qualified in your mind. What's your evidence? Do we have to accept that everyone from Berkeley is outstanding? Are you saying his pedigree is a proxy for his competence?

Professor A: Why not? And, listen, Walter will hit the ground running and fit in very easily here. You certainly can't say that about the other three finalists. And remember that I said Latorya's nervousness during the first five minutes of her job talk was really revealing to me. 'Thumbs down' is what I say for her if she's going to be shaking in her boots.

Professor B: Hey, just because you're so over-confident doesn't mean that everyone else has to be. Just remember that Latorya, unlike the other candidates, had been trapped at O'Hare by the blizzard and arrived only <u>ten</u> minutes before her talk was scheduled. I myself would have been speechless at that point. Look: I think Latorya's letters of recommendation are very persuasive and detailed. Her law degree is from Emory University. Her letter-writers made a point of underscoring how resourceful she's been and really how 'over-productive' she's been at Emory. And remember they mentioned the rather modest background of her original family. I think that speaks volumes for her toughness and for ability to inspire our students.

Professor A: My gosh, this begins to sound like the special pleadings of a do-gooder social worker. Pleaaassse, save me all this. In order to have credibility, we've got to make sure we hire only from a very prestigious place. We can't veer from that, even though it wasn't officially one of our selection criterion. We can't afford to lose face with our colleagues, within and outside our department. And besides, I don't know any of the so-called experts who have vouched for Latorya—not even one. That's a bad sign, for sure.

Chair: I can't understand why you're so adamant that Latorya must be from a 'top tier' place in order to be taken seriously. If she were a European-American man with a Midwest accent, would you be so adamant? I sense that you're maybe uneasy about Latorya's trappings or, I don't know, her personal style. Is that right? I've heard nothing negative from you about her scholarship and teaching, either past achievements or future promise. So what gives?

Professor A: Well, it's just that we've never had an African American—let alone a minority woman—in our department. We have to be very, very careful because we could get burned. Even though I like her writing samples and her teaching evaluations, I'm just a bit uneasy about her fit. And if we hire her, I predict that some of the others in our department will feel uneasy and, you know, awkward and confused about how to act. That's relevant, isn't it?   END.

REFERENCES

Ancona, D. et al. *Managing for the Future: Organizational Behavior and Processes*. Cincinatti, Ohio: South-Western Publishing Co., 1999.

Bauer, C. and B. Baltes. "Reducing the Effects of Gender Stereotypes on Performance Evaluations." *Sex Roles* 47, Nos. 9/10 (2002): 465-74.

Benjamin, L. *The Black Elite: Facing the Color Line in the Twilight of the Twentieth Century*. Chicago: Nelson-Hall, 1998.

Biernat, M. "Toward a Broader View of Social Stereotyping." *American Psychologist*. Vol. 58, No.12 (2003): 1019-1027.

Blair, I. and M. Banaji. "Automatic and Controlled Processes in Stereotype Priming." *Journal of Personality and Social Psychology*. 1996: Vol. 60, No. 6, 1142-1163.

Bond, W. "Using Simulation to Instruct Emergency Medicine Residents in Cognitive Forcing Strategies." *Academic Medicine* 79 (2004):438-446.

Cooper, J. and D. Stevens, eds. *Tenure in the Sacred Grove: Issues and Strategies for Women and Minority Faculty*. Albany: State University of New York Press, 2002.

Croskerry, P. "The Importance of Cognitive Errors in Diagnosis and Strategies to Minimize Them." *Academic Medicine* 78(2003): 775-780.

Dahl, R. *How Democratic is the American Constitution?* New Haven, CT: Yale University Press, 2001.

Dawson, V. and H. Arkes. "Systematic Errors in Medical Decision Making: Judgment Limitations." *Journal of General Internal Medicine* 1987; 2L 183-187.

Delgado, R. "Mexican Americans as a Legally Cognizable Class." In *The Latino/a Condition*, ed. R. Delgado and J. Stefancic. New York: New York University Press, 1998.

Dettmar, K. "What We Waste When Faculty Hiring Goes Wrong." *Chronicle of Higher Education*. Dec. 17, 2004, pp. B6-B8.

Fair, B. *Notes of a Racial Caste Baby: Color Blindness and the End of Affirmative Action*. New York: New York University Press, 1997.

Fischer, C., et al. *Inequality by Design: Cracking the Bell Curve Myth*. Princeton: Princeton University Press, 1996.

Foschi, M. "Gender and Double Standards for Competence." In C. L. Ridgeway (ed.), *Gender, Interaction, and Inequality*, pp. 181-207. New York: Springer-Verlag, 1992.

Frank, F. "Taking Up a Professorial Line at Florida A&M University." In *Affirmed Action: Essays on the Academic and Social Lives of White Faculty Members at HBCUs*, ed. L. Forster, J. Guydes, and A. Miller. Lanham, MD: Towman and Littlefield, 1999.

Fried, L., et al. "Career Development for Women in Academic Medicine: Multiple Interventions in a Department of Medicine." *Journal of the American Medical Association* 276 (9/18/1996): 898-905.

Gallos, J. and J. Ramsey. *Teaching Diversity*. San Francisco: Jossey Bass, 1997.

Garcia, M. ed. *Succeeding in an Academic Career: A Guide for Faculty of Color*. Westport, CT: Greenwood Press, 2000.

Greenwald, A. & L. Krieger. "Implicit Bias: Scientific Foundations." *California Law Review*. 2006; 94: 945-965.

Groopman, J. *How Doctors Think*. New York: Houghton Mifflin, 2007.

Guinier, L. and G. Torres. The *Miner's Canary: Enlisting Race, Resisting Power, Transforming Democracy.* Cambridge, MA: Harvard University Press, 2002.

Kahneman, D. "Bounded Rationality: A Perspective on Judgment and Choice." *American Psychologist* 58, No.9 (2003): 697-720.

Kanter, R. *Men and Women of the Corporation*. New York: Basic Books, 1997.

Kobrynowicz, D. and M. Biernat. "Decoding Subjective Evaluations: How Stereotypes Provide Shifting Standards." *Journal of Experimental Social Psychology*. 33 (1997): 579-601.

Kunda, Z., L. Sinclair, and D. Griffin. "Equal Ratings but Separate Meanings: Stereotypes and the Construal of Traits." *Journal of Personality and Social Psychology* 103 (1997): 720-34.

Lee, Y. "Koreans in Japan and the United States." In *Minority Status and Schooling: A Comparative Study of Immigrant and Involuntary Minorities,* edited by J. Ogbu and M. Gibson. New York: Garland, 1991.

Lopez, I. "Colorblind to the Reality of Race in America." *Chronicle of Higher Education Review* Nov. 3, 2006: pp. B6-B8.

Madera, J., M. Hebl, & R. Martin. "Gender and Letters of Recommendation for Academia: Agentic and Communal Differences." *Journal of Applied Psychology* 94 (2009): 1591-1599.

Martell, R., D. Lane, and C. Emrich. "Male-Female Differences: A Computer Simulation." *American Psychologist* 51 (1991):157-58.

Martell, R. "Sex Bias at Work: The Effects of Attentional and Memory Demands on Performance Ratings for Men and Women*." Journal of Applied Social Psychology* 21 (1991): 1939-60.

McIntosh, P. "White Privilege: Unpacking the Invisible Knapsack." *Peace and Freedom* (July/August 1989): 10-14.

Mervis, J. "New Data in Chemistry Show 'Zero' Diversity." *Science* 292 (2001): 1291.

MIT Faculty Newsletter, March 1999, web.mit.edu/fnl/women/women.html. Updates on gender equity at MIT appear periodically at this website.

Moody, J. *Faculty Diversity: Problems and Solutions*. New York: Routledge, 2004.

Moore, W. and L. Wagstaff. *Black Educators in White Colleges*. San Francisco: Jossey-Bass, 1974.

Morrison, A., R. White, and E. Van Velsor. *Breaking the Glass Ceiling: Why Women Don't Reach the Top of Large Corporations*. Reading, MA: Addison-Wesley, 1992.

Moskowitz, G., P. Gollwitzer, and W. Wasel. "Preconscious Control of Stereotype Activation Through Chronic Egalitarian Goals." *Journal of Personality and Social Psychology*. Vol. 77, No. 1, 167-184. July 1999

Nahavandi, A., and A. Malekzadeh. *Organizational Behavior: The Person-Organization Fit*. Upper Saddle River, NJ: Prentice Hall, 1999.

Nelson, D. and J. Quick. *Organizational Behavior: Foundations, Realities, and Challenges*. Mason, Ohio: South-Western, 2003.

O'Rourke, S. "What Can Be Done: Race and Gender-Neutral Strategies for Increasing Faculty Diversity," paper distributed at the "Keeping Our Faculties" National Conference, University of Minnesota, Minneapolis, Nov. 2004.

Phelps. E. et al (2000). "Performance on Indirect Measures of Race Evaluation Predicts Amygdala Activation." *Journal of Cognitive Neuroscience* 12(5): 729-738.

Padilla, R. and R. Chavez, eds. The *Leaning Ivory Tower: Latino Professors in American Universities*. Albany: State University of New York Press, 1995.

Payne, D. "Bridging the Gender Gap: How to Stop Women Leaving Research." *Electronic ("E") Magazine of the European Life Scientist*. Issue 12, Dec. 2002.

Pinker, S. *The Blank Slate*. New York: Viking Press, 2002.

Rains, F. "Is the Benign Really Harmless?" In *White Reign: Deploying Whiteness in America*, edited by J. Kincheloe et al. New York: St. Martin's Griffin Press. 1998.

------. "Dancing on the Sharp Edge of the Sword: Women Faculty of Color in White Academe." In *Everyday Knowledge and Uncommon Truths,* edited by L. Smith and K. Kellor. Boulder: Westview Press, 1999.

Redelmeier, D. "The Cognitive Psychology of Missed Diagnoses." *Annals of Internal Medicine* 142 (2005): 115-120.

Reiss, S. "Nell Painter: Making It as a Woman of Color in the Academy." *Diversity Digest*, Fall 1997, 6-7.

Rosser, S. *The Science Glass Ceiling*. New York: Routledge, 2004.

Sagaria, M. "An Exploratory Model of Filtering in Administrative Searches: Toward Counter-Hegemonic Discourses." *Journal of Higher Education* 73 (2002): 677-704.

Sanchirico, C. "Evidence, Procedure, and the Upside of Cognitive Errors." *Stanford Law Review* 57(2004): 291-330.

Smith, D. *Achieving Faculty Diversity: Debunking the Myths*. Washington, D.C.: Association of American Colleges and Universities, 1996.

------. "How to Diversify the Faculty." *Academe*, Sept.-Oct. 2000, 48-52.

Springer, A. "How to Diversify Faculty: The Current Legal Landscape." Paper published by American Association of University Professors and distributed at the National Conference on Race and Ethnicity in Higher Education, San Francisco, June 2004.

Steele, C., and J. Aronson. "Stereotype Threat and the Intellectual Test Performance of African Americans. *Journal of Personality and Social Psychology* 69 (1995): 797-811.   Also see www.ReduceStereotypeThreat.com.

Sturm, S. and L. Guinier. "The Future of Affirmative Action: Reclaiming the Innovative Ideal." *California Law Review* 84 (1996): 953-1036.

Sunstein, D. and R. Thaler. *Nudge: Improving Decisions about Health, Wealth, and Happiness*. New Haven: Yale University Press, 2008.

Takaki, R. "To Count or Not to Count By Race and Gender?" In *From Different Shores: Perspectives on Race and Ethnicity in America*, edited by R. Takaki. New York: Oxford University Press, 1987.

------. *Strangers from a Different Shore, A History of Asian Americans*. Boston: Little, Brown, 1989.

------. *A Different Mirror: A History of Multicultural America*. Boston: Little, Brown, 1993.

Tenure Denied: Cases of Sex Discrimination in Academia. Washington, D.C.: American Association of University Women Educational Foundation and AAUW Legal Advocacy Fund, 2004.

Trix, F., and C. Psenka. "Exploring the Color of Glass: Letters of Recommendation for Female and Male Medical Faculty." *Discourse & Society* 14 (2003): 191-220.

Trower, C., and R. Chait. "Faculty Diversity: Too Little for Too Long." *Harvard Magazine*, March-April 2002, 33-36. [At the website www.harvard-magazine.com are data tables that accompany Trower's and Chait's article.]

Turner, C. *Diversifying the Faculty: A Guidebook for Search Committees*. Washington, D.C.: Association of American Colleges and Universities, 2002.

University of Michigan Faculty Work-Life Study Report. Ann Arbor: University of Michigan, 1999.

Valian, V. "Sex, Schemas, and Success: What's Keeping Women Back?" *Academe*, Sept. 1998, 50-5.

------. *Why So Slow? The Advancement of Women*. Cambridge, MA: MIT Press, 1998.

Wade, K., and A.Kinicki. "Examining Objective and Subjective Applicant Qualifications within a Process Model of Interview Selection Decisions." *Academy of Management Journal* 38 (1995): 151-55.

Wenneras, C., and A. Wold. "Nepotism and Sexism in Peer Review." *Nature* 387 (1997): 341-43.

Wenneras, C., and A. Wold. "A Chair of One's Own: The Upper Reaches of Academe Remain Stubbornly Inaccessible to Women." *Nature* 408 (2000): 647.

Whetten, D. and K. Cameron. *Developing Management Skills*. Upper Saddle River, N.J.: Prentice Hall, 2002.

Williams, C.G. *Technology and the Dream: Reflections on the Black Experience at MIT, 1941-1999*. Cambridge, MA: MIT Press, 2001.

Williams, C.L. "The Glass Escalator: Hidden Advantages for Men in the 'Female' Professions." *Social Problems* 39 (1992): 253-67.

Wilson, T. and N. Brekke. "Mental Contamination and Mental Correction: Unwanted Influences on Judgments and Evaluations." *Psychological Bulletin* 116 (1994): 117-42.

"Women Make Gains in Getting Canadian Research Chairs." *Chronicle of Higher Education*, Nov. 26, 2004, p. A38.

Wu, F. *Yellow: Race in America Beyond Black and White*. New York: Basic Books, 2002.

MAJOR POINTS IN "RISING ABOVE COGNITIVE ERRORS"
Copyright JoAnn Moody, 2010 www.DiversityOnCampus.com

Part I. Typical Cognitive Errors Unwittingly Made by Individuals

1. Negative stereotyping/biases
2. Positive stereotyping/biases
3. Raising the bar; Shifting standards
4. Elitism; Academic pedigree
5. First impressions
6. Longing to clone
7. Good fit/Bad fit & other "trump cards"
8. Provincialism
9. Assumptions/"psychoanalyzing the candidate"
10. Wishful thinking/personal opinions
11. Self-fulfilling prophecy
12. Seizing a pretext
13. Character over context
14. Premature ranking/Digging in
15. Yielding to momentum of the group

Typical Dysfunctions of an Organization that Exacerbate Cognitive Errors

1. Overloading/rushing
2. No coaching and practice
3. No ground rules
4. No reminders and monitoring
5. No one held accountable
6. No debriefing and systematic improvement

Part II. How to Rise Above Cognitive Errors & Remedy Organizational Dysfunctions

1. Constant self-correction by individuals and evaluation committees
2. Coaching and follow-up reminders and nudges about how to guard against cognitive errors, personal opinions, shortcuts, and "trump cards." Tips from respected peers. Check on-line tutorial for search committees at: virginia.edu/vpfa/search.html   Also check: www.implicit.harvard.edu
3. Ground rules and checklists to govern the evaluation process, developed by the committee (but consult guidelines from previous evaluations or from outside experts)
4. Diverse committee, including professor from another department.   A Process Monitor on the committee for quality control and to assist committee chair in insuring careful and opinion-free deliberations
5. Use a matrix or other visual aid to keep evaluation criteria front and center
6. Slow down the evaluation and decision-making process; no overloading or rushing
7. Build accountability into both processes and results and use a variety of checklists
8. Lengthen interviews and use simulations to get a fuller picture of applicants
9. Don't rank the finalists. Instead, write up a summary of each one's strengths, weaknesses, and likely contributions to students, patients, clients, the department, and the school
10. Avoid a solo situation by including two or more members of negatively stereotyped groups in the pool of finalists
11. Continuously practice so that self-correction and prevention of cognitive errors become long-term cognitive habits (through case studies, interactive skits, formal observation by others, checklists, debriefing after evaluations and decisions have been reached)
12. Develop personal relationships/friendships with members of negatively stereotyped groups—to diminish social distance and automatic stereotyping
13. Frequent insistence on "Show me the evidence" during evaluation processes
14. Debrief after each search or evaluation; aim for quality-control and improvement; provide summaries of lessons learned, for future committees and leaders.

DR. MOODY'S NATIONAL CONSULTING PRACTICE

How My Consulting Work in Academia is Unique:

❖ **I deal interactively with power-holders (presidents, provosts, deans, department chairs, search committees, faculty senates, trustees)** at large and small campuses and professional schools of law, medicine, business, and engineering. In *problem-based sessions and retreats,* I tap into the wisdom brought to the table by power-holders: I actively engage them in identifying blocks to faculty and student diversity and in brainstorming how to remove the blocks. As the analysis and brainstorming proceed, I share strategies and caveats derived from my consulting and research. Participants, with my assistance, develop or refine *action plans* for improved recruitment, retention, mentorship, and peer review at their campuses and professional schools.

❖ **As an external expert, I assist diversity officers and faculty developers in advancing their goals**. At times, it is strategically wise to have an outside expert provide new perspectives and caveats regarding how goals are currently being implemented. Schools also benefit from learning about the successful experiences of other institutions. To insure that change-making continues, I frequently *train [internal] trainers* to sustain the momentum.

❖ **Working with mentoring programs,** I coach mentors and department chairs on how to: deal with *critical incidents* frequently experienced by their mentees; reduce the stressors that mentees face if they are *solos* (the only one or one of only a few women or under-represented minority faculty or students in an academic setting); *frontload* all new faculty hires with extra attention and encouragement so they feel they belong and are more likely to thrive. I run mentor- and mentee-readiness workshops as well as help build quality-control mechanisms into newly formed and established mentoring programs designed for post-doctoral scholars and early-stage faculty.

❖ **For early-stage faculty (pre-tenure, research-only, tenure-track, adjunct, physician/faculty, term, clinical-only, and so on) as well as post-docs and future faculty,** I lead demystifying sessions on how they can more effectively maximize their success and satisfaction in academe.

Typical Areas of My Consulting Work:

❖ Improving recruitment, retention, mentorship, and evaluation of faculty, students, post-docs, and staff (especially women and under-represented minorities who are frequently *solos*)

❖ Removing contaminants and cognitive errors from search, peer-review, and other evaluation processes (errors which often disproportionately hurt women and minorities being evaluated)

❖ Recognizing and replacing dysfunctional departmental practices and assumptions

❖ Frontloading all early-stage faculty with support and collegiality to ensure their retention

❖ Building a cadre of faculty and staff advocates or equity advisors for campus diversity.

Comments on Dr. Moody's Consulting Work:

❖ *Dr. Moody has developed excellent materials and approaches that engage deans, chairs, search committees, and others in analyzing problem-based scenarios and then developing remedies and action plans.* **President Bud Peterson, Georgia Tech (former Chancellor, UCO-Boulder and former Provost, RPI)**

❖ *JoAnn Moody brings exceptional expertise, warmth, and effectiveness to her consulting practice. I am delighted that professional schools are beginning to tap into her wisdom and use her publications.* **Christopher K.R.T. Jones, Guthridge Professor of Mathematics and former Department Chair, UNC-Chapel Hill (former Professor, Brown University).**

ABOUT THE AUTHOR

As a long-time national specialist in faculty development and diversity, I have helped campuses and professional schools rethink and improve: recruitment, mentorship, evaluation, and retention of faculty, students, and staff, especially women and minorities. Using my experience as a college professor and consortium vice president, I have consulted with: senior administrators, faculty groups, diversity officers and councils, search and tenure review committees, faculty developers, mentoring program officers, and trustees. I also have organized "demystifying" workshops for tenure-track and adjunct faculty as well as for post-doctoral scholars, future faculty, and graduate students.

My clients have included: Cornell, Purdue, Kansas State, Texas A&M, New Mexico State, RPI, Case Western, Carnegie Mellon, UCLA, Rutgers, La Verne, Virginia, Southern California, Washington, New Hampshire, Alabama, Colorado, Texas, Claremont Graduate School & Colleges, Michigan Tech, Rochester, Wisconsin, Florida, UNC Chapel Hill & others. Also medical schools: Stanford, UC Irvine, Toronto, Calgary & others. Also colleges: Allegheny, Macalester, Middlebury, Mt. Holyoke, Keene State, Smith, Northern Essex Community College, & the Riverside (CA) Community College District.

Comments about "Rising Above Cognitive Errors":

"Dr. Moody's publication is of enormous practical benefit for any academic organization. She provides a catalog of cognitive errors that can inadvertently sabotage our various personnel processes and gives the practical tools to minimize them." **Terry King, Provost, Ball State University and former Dean of Engineering, Kansas State University.**

"I understand why professional schools, universities, and colleges would distribute hundreds of copies of this exceptional publication and organize follow-up discussions with various committees and leaders—just as the Provost's Office at the University of Florida has done." **Debra Walker King, Associate Provost for Faculty Development and Professor of English, University of Florida.**

Dr. Moody is the author of:

Faculty Diversity: Removing the Barriers, Second Edition (2012). This book may be ordered from Routledge Press or Amazon.com. [*"Those already dedicated to the project of faculty diversity will be fortified, renewed, and energized. Cynics and skeptics may yet be persuaded there* are *real solutions. We cannot afford to ignore this book."* Evelyn Hu-DeHart, Professor of History and Director, Center for the Study of Race and Ethnicity in America, Brown University]

Dr. Moody's other practical booklets:

Demystifying the Profession: Helping Early-Stage Faculty Succeed (Resources for Medical, Law, & Business Schools and Colleges & Universities). with Discussion Scenarios for practice, revised 2010. Used by faculty affairs, orientation organizers, leadership- and mentor-development programs, chairs, deans, post-docs, medical residents, and early-stage faculty.

Mentoring Early-Stage Faculty at Colleges, Universities, & Professional Schools (Resources for Mentors & Mentees; Provosts, Deans, & Department Chairs; Organizers & Evaluators of Formal Mentoring Programs, with Discussion Scenarios for practice, revised 2010. Mentoring is widely viewed as essential but often provided in sporadic and superficial ways. This booklet aims to remedy such shortcomings. Readiness workshops for mentors and mentees are outlined. Checklists for chairs, provosts, deans, and mentors are included.

"Solo" Faculty at Colleges, Universities, & Professional Schools: Improving Retention & Reducing Stress (Resources for Departments & their Chairs, Deans, Mentors, Faculty Developers, & Solos Themselves), with Discussion Scenarios (practice exercises); revised 2010. Women and minorities in "skewed-ratio" departments can find themselves dealing with several stressors. Interventions are necessary.

Made in the USA
Columbia, SC
25 May 2018